Is Your Business Sick?

How to Identify, Diagnose & Cure
Parasites Infecting Your Business
So It Can Grow from Sick to Successful

is your

How to Identify, Diagnose & Cure

business

Parasites Infecting Your Business

sick?

So It Can Grow from Sick to Successful

Gary & Susan Harper

Published by Sharper Business Solutions.

IN LOVING MEMORY

Dianne Robinson
1956-2019

This book is dedicated to Dianne Robinson,
whose joy was limitless and whose happiness
knew no bounds. During our struggles she would
remind us that "joy can heal the body."

Thank you, Mom, for all you were and all you gave.

"A merry heart doeth good like a medicine:
but a broken spirit drieth the bones."

Proverbs 17:22 KJV

Table of Contents

Introduction

Is Your Business Sick is the result of our deeply personal and terrifying experience of my (Gary) dealing with a chronic illness I didn't know I had. Our experience with discovering the parasite, getting it diagnosed, and figuring out how to treat and recover from it provides the foundation for the guidance in this book. Through the process we discovered similar parallels in businesses that were suffering from some kind of "illness," and we started seeing ways that we could help businesses identify the metaphoric parasites that were killing their businesses from the inside out. Following is the story of what led us to this discovery of the illness, what we endured on the road to recovery, and, ultimately, how this book was born, told from Gary's perspective.

The Struggle Began

It was 2012. I had just won a prestigious award presented by the Fortune 500 company I worked for. I had recently lost ninety pounds and was in the best shape of my life. Susan and I were happy, our children, Annemarie and Jacob, were thriving, and life was good.

I woke up one Saturday morning and felt a little off. Susan was gone for a girls' weekend with her mom and sisters. As I laid in bed alone it felt like the room was spinning. My head hurt and I was confused and groggy, as if I hadn't slept in a very long time. I told myself it was because I had gotten more sleep than usual and decided to get up and start my day with a hot shower. Then things went from bad to worse.

In the shower I got so dizzy I thought I was going to faint—twice. After the third dizzy spell that almost took me to my knees passed, I shut off the water and got out. Then my heart started pounding and all the muscles in my body tightened up. I made it to the floor without falling then began to experience what I thought was a seizure. I called for my son, Jacob, who came in, covered me up with a towel, then ran to our neighbor, Damian's, house. Damian was a police officer. He called the paramedics then came over to stay with me until the paramedics arrived and rushed me to the hospital.

At the hospital, doctors ran test after test to try to determine the cause of what was happening. Susan got there and for the next four hours we anxiously waited for the test results. We were stunned when the doctors told us all of my test results looked great and they didn't see a reason for my episode. The only result that was slightly off was that my blood sugar was a little low, so the doctor said that was probably the cause for why I felt the way I did physically, which then seemed to lead me to having a panic attack. We had no reason to think anything different. I felt so silly, like I'd overreacted, was grateful for the seemingly good news, and couldn't wait to get home. But this was just the beginning of strange symptoms, test results that didn't show anything wrong, and a long uphill battle to save my own life.

While I continued to feel off for the next few days, I chalked that up to continuing to struggle with low blood sugar. I altered my diet a bit and hoped for the best. By that Friday,

I started to feel like I had the flu, but I pushed those symptoms aside because I was so excited to get home from work and coach Jacob's first championship baseball game.

I left work around three for the ninety minute commute from Chicago. But with each step through the parking lot to my car, the same symptoms I had experienced a week earlier in the shower returned. Fear flooded my mind and panic gripped me. I tried to calm myself down, telling myself I had to be stronger than "just another panic attack." I made it to my car and started to drive. After a few minutes, though, I knew something was terribly wrong and that this was not just a panic attack. I called Susan who told me to pull over and call 911. Unable to think clearly, I did as she instructed and once again found myself being rushed to the hospital.

After waiting for almost two hours, I started to feel better physically, and my sense of obligation to be at my son's game weighed heavily on me. I wanted so badly to be there for him. We left the hospital and made it to his game. Though I couldn't coach or even walk to the field, I watched him from the car in the parking lot. We had no idea that this was just the beginning of a life of limitations.

The Struggle Continues

I was thirty-five years old and at the peak of my professional success. But what we were referring to as panic attacks kept happening more and more frequently. At one point I was having up to fifteen a day. The situation was becoming unbearable. I went to doctor after doctor, all of whom said my bloodwork was fine, that panic attacks were normal, and I just needed to figure out a way to reduce my stress to deal with them. But we couldn't accept that answer and no matter what we did, I wasn't getting better.

We spent the next six months and our entire savings trying to get to the root of the problem. I kept asking: What is causing this? Why is this disruption happening in my life? Why am I so sick? During this time, new and increasingly more frightening symptoms appeared. My cognitive function started to decline and with it, my independence, which I had always been so proud of. I was unable to work full time and could no longer drive. I was frustrated, depressed, and in debt from all the medical expenses I'd accumulated, all to get the same answer: there was nothing wrong with me. Four months later I had to take a medical leave of absence from my job. Then, finally, we found our answer. But our journey was far from over.

The Diagnosis

We found a doctor located in northwest Indiana named Dr. Mike Streeter. He told me that I had an illness called Lyme disease, which is caused by a tick bite. He explained that the disease had overrun my body and I was considered as a "late-stage" case, which is very hard to treat. He said that we needed to extract this infection and the parasites from my body. My long road to recovery stretched ahead of us.

When someone goes through treatment for Lyme disease, their body reacts to the dying off of the bacteria and parasites inside them with what is called a Jarisch-Herxheimer reaction. So the process of getting well involves getting a whole lot sicker first, making it a difficult, frustrating, and depressing process. At this point, though, we had no choice but to trust the process, a lesson we would take with us into our professional lives in the future, though we didn't know yet just how meaningful a lesson it would be.

Though I finally knew why I was sick, what I was sick with, and I had a plan to extract the parasites and get well, I was forced to find ways to combat what the disease was taking from me. I had to come up with creative solutions to work on my memory, which continued to fade, so each night I would record what I had learned that day so I could refer back to it the next day. I had to resist getting complacent and giving up, so I committed to working on myself spiritually. I knew I needed to do things to help myself fight this disease and get well. It wasn't easy, but I wanted to get well for myself and for my family.

Then one day I found myself sitting across from a church counselor. I was completely depleted and, feeling like I had nothing left to give, I simply surrendered. I surrendered to feeling ill, exhausted, and lost. I stopped (for just a moment) trying to figure everything out. The relief I experienced was extraordinary. In that moment I experienced God's perfect love and I was fully present. I believe this was the real first step on my journey to truly becoming well.

Is Your Business Sick?

As I continued treatment and began feeling better, Susan and I started noticing some connections between businesses that weren't running well—that seemed "sick"—and some of my experiences with being ill. We came to the conclusion that businesses can also host an infection or a parasite, just like my body had, and that if those infections weren't extracted, the business would eventually become so sick it would die.

What we realized is that parasites in businesses come in three forms—the business owner, the staff, and/or in various types of distractions. We've helped many businesses—both in corporate America and small- to mid-sized companies—and time again we've seen this parallel between a business being "sick" and it having one or more of the parasites we started identifying. One of the main reasons people hire us is because they have parasites in their business—even though they don't know it.

We have divided this book into three sections to help you identify some of the parasites that exist in business, starting with owners, moving to staff, then covering distractions. We use stories and anecdotes as "the diagnosis" to help illustrate the symptoms of certain parasites we have seen in businesses, then we offer a cure to help you take the necessary steps to rid your business of the parasite.

Remember, though, most people do not think of themselves as parasites and are not accustomed to thinking of others in this way, either. As a result, identifying a parasite can have some very real, emotional complications. Just as I had to endure going through a treatment that made me feel worse so I could get better, dealing with a parasite in your business is challenging, frustrating, and painful. But doing the hard work necessary to thrive will yield a business that can and will be fruitful, profitable, and—most important—healthy.

Our goal for *Is Your Business Sick?* is to help readers first identify and diagnose illness in their businesses, then give them the tools they need—the cure—to recover, so that their businesses will not only continue to grow in a healthy capacity but also will be well enough to avoid falling prey to another sickness in the future. We hope that readers will become educated and empowered so that they can grow their businesses from sick to successful.

Part One

Are You the Parasite?

As you now know from our experience with Gary's illness, sometimes our bodies can be infected with an illness and we don't even know it. The same is true with businesses. And sometimes we as the business owners are being a parasite on our businesses, causing them to be sick and limiting their growth. This isn't always malicious or intentional, and our goal is to help you identify those behaviors or mindsets that you may have that are making your business ill so that you can effectively recover from them and move on to being successful and healthy.

If you discover that you have been a parasite in your own business, this does not mean that the situation is fatal. By applying the cures outlined here, you can overcome the illness. You can choose to make positive changes in your life and the way you do business that will alter its trajectory so it can grow from sick to successful.

Are You Draining Your Company's Resources?

Most entrepreneurs need to expand and grow their businesses, part of which is being able to hire more people, to expand your processes, to create automation, and so forth. Simply, it's needing to be able to spend money in order to grow. One of the very first symptoms of someone draining their company's resources is that there's no money available to reinvest in the company.

Likewise, we see some entrepreneurs who don't have a budget and who don't put the business first. They manage the finances just enough to ensure there's money to pay themselves, their staff, and their vendors/contractors, but they don't leave cash in the business to take care of the inevitable emergencies that will arise or to plan for expansion and future growth.

We often refer to the business as "Mama" and we say, "If Mama ain't happy, ain't nobody happy." If you're not paying Mama first, even before you pay yourself, then your business could suffer. Many entrepreneurs are functioning from a place of reactivity instead of proactivity, meaning that they are failing to plan for the future and are essentially using their businesses like ATMs—money comes in, money goes out.

Part of this parasite of draining your business's resources and using it as an ATM is a mindset problem. Some entrepreneurs have an entitlement mindset and they hold this belief that "As long as the bills are being paid, I should be able to have whatever I want and buy whatever I want." But this short-sighted thinking can end up costing the business greatly in the long run. We always say that if you fail to plan, then you plan to fail. Using your business like a cash machine is setting your-self up for failure. As a business owner, if you're destroying your company by taking too much cash and using it as a cash machine, you're effectively being a parasite on your own busi-ness by draining it of the valuable resources it needs to not only survive, but to thrive and be healthy in all financial climates.

The Diagnosis

John was a smart business owner whose product was in high demand. In his first year of business, John committed to paying off old debts as a way to ensure his new business had a good name. He opted to only focus on keeping the business afloat enough to pay his debts off. While his product was doing well, John watched his business grow forty percent year over year. He didn't budget for the future, he didn't invest any money back into the company, and if there was a time where there seemed like there wasn't going to be enough money to cover his debt payments, he'd quickly try to find a new deal or a new client to work with to cover those expenses. He didn't think about or plan for eventually needing to expand his business to keep up with his competition.

Unfortunately, John underestimated the time this would take and the impact this decision would have on his business's health. By the fifth year, John's company was in a position to pay off the remaining balance of his old debt. But, halfway through that year, John reviewed his bi-annual P&L statement and noticed a few problems that he did not have the financial resources to take care of: High labor expenses were eating up his profits. Product defects were costing his business rework. And there were additional costs associated with replacing the defective product that he didn't plan on.

John's decision to drain the business of cash during its profitable years was now coming back to hurt his company and jeopardize the legacy he was hoping to build for his family and the employees that trusted him to ensure a stable financial environment. After finally looking at his numbers and seeing exactly the predicament he was in, John's business was poised to take a loss of over $500,000.

The Cure

This parasite of stealing money or robbing the wealth from your own business can be a detriment to your business. It may not look like it in the moment, as was the case with John, but if you don't leave money in the business, you have nothing to fall back on during hard times. We always tell people that if they will keep three to six months' worth of cash on hand in their companies, they'll keep their businesses healthy and protected in the downtimes. Part of paying "Mama" is making sure that you have at least ninety days' worth of cash in an emergency fund.

In order to do this, you need to have good financial data: good budgets, good P&L's, and a good bookkeeper who you meet with *regularly*—at least monthly, ideally weekly. And you must have a budget that accounts for making payments to Mama. Plan to pay the business to create those reserve funds. That isn't "leftover" money, it's money that goes to Mama, not because the business needs it right now, but because you'll have it in the future when there's an emergency. And, this strategy sets you up so that you're not counting on future profits to pay today's expenses.

Part of creating your budget is having an understanding about your numbers. You need to know what your revenues are, what your expenses are, and how much you should be spending. You must determine what Mama needs in order for the business to at the very least be sustainable and, eventually, to grow. In addition, within your identified expenses you need to create a budget around personnel. And, yes, you need to pay yourself, but you must pay yourself like you would an employee, and avoid using your business as your personal ATM. Those resources are not there to be used on shiny objects like cars and vacations. They are there to keep your business alive, healthy, and thriving.

Part of your budget work is also developing accountability. Many entrepreneurs hate looking at their numbers, but you must face any fears you may have and look at your metrics regularly. Doing so is a crucial step in planning for your business's success. Once you have your budgets in place, you need to review them monthly. Part of the accountability process is ensuring that any variances you see in the numbers are fully explored and explained so you know why and can make any necessary adjustments.

Again, failing to plan is planning to fail. If you think of your business as a personal ATM and drain its resources, you are hindering its growth and being a parasite, which will only lead to failure.

Are You Limiting Your Business By Not Letting Go?

At the start of any business, the owners have to work numerous hours both *in* and *on* the business. This is an important distinction because at some point you need to only be doing one or the other and those entrepreneurs who are trying to do both all the time are being parasites, infecting their business from within and stunting it so it cannot grow.

When you start a small company you can take advantage of being a resource that can work both in and on it. By this we mean you'll likely be doing tasks that range in monetary value if you were paying someone else to do them, from $10/hour tasks up to several hundred dollar an hour tasks. At the outset, you'll likely be arranging your own meetings, taking and making sales calls, creating contracts, and so forth. Each of these tasks is an "in the business" kind of task.

Your job at the beginning will also include sub-seats like IT, office management, receptionist, and any other role you have to take to protect the sales, products, customers, and financial health of the business. When we talk about working "on the business" we are referring to other tasks like building a vision, planning for growth and moving forward, and overseeing effective systems for the four major departments within an organization. You may find yourself being the CEO, COO, marketing manager, sales manager, operations manager, finance manager, and many other titles, all at the same time.

Most business owners will perform in each of these seats just long enough to create success, and then they will start replacing themselves in the seats they don't like or are not that good at. This is the proper way to grow. Effective delegation ensures the health of your business. How effectively an owner delegates tasks, responsibilities, and entire positions to more skilled individuals, the stronger the company becomes.

If you as the owner are delegating only positions to other employees, but not the *responsibilities* that come with the position, then you are a parasite infecting your business and limiting its health and potential. By holding onto positions you shouldn't be, you are inhibiting your business's growth and success, which will eventually lead to its death. Often, our egos keep us from delegating. The very thing that makes us successful, driven, and what we draw upon to propel us to the next level can also be what is stunting our overall business success and growth.

When we step away from trying to manage everything and from trying to sit in every seat, we free ourselves up for unlimited growth, instead of capping that growth by trying to do everything ourselves—and likely only doing some of it well. When we can push down that ego and say, "Hey, I can't be everything to everybody, and I can't sit in every seat in my company," then we are removing the invisible cap that inhibits growth and makes our businesses sick.

The Diagnosis

Fred was a very successful solopreneur whose business grew rapidly in its first year. Fred worked tirelessly in his business. As it was growing, he sat in many seats and saw a lot of success. He also saw his share of failure, which ultimately enabled him to perfect his product and service for each of his clients. Eventually, though, Fred got overwhelmed by doing everything himself, and even started getting complaints from his customers because they couldn't reach him like they used to. Fred knew it was time to hire some support staff.

Fred's first hire was in finance, which was an area of weakness for him. He brought in Beth, a bookkeeper, to relieve him of this burden that he didn't enjoy and wasn't particularly skilled at. Within three months Beth was fully trained and was even going above and beyond her role to suggest process improvements. Fred saw the value in delegating tasks to Beth and even gave her some other areas of the business to fill her capacity and reduce his.

Since Beth was doing so well in her role, Fred decided to bring in a sales manager to focus on business growth. After a few rounds of interviews Fred hired Jacob, who he felt would be the best fit for the business. Within thirty days Jacob was trained on the sales process and was delivering results. Three months into his employment, Jacob had increased the company sales by twenty percent. Fred was happy with the growth of the business and the team who was supporting it.

In the face of their respective success, both Beth and Jacob started to notice a frustrating occurrence. Each on separate occasions would go to perform a task specific to their roles only to discover that it had already been done. At one point, Jacob followed up with a lead and found out that Fred had already contacted them. Beth contacted the accountant to request a report she needed and was told that Fred had requested the same report only hours prior. At first Beth and Jacob let these seemingly minor irritations roll off their backs, but then it started happening regularly.

One day Fred stopped Jacob in the hall to tell him that he'd been working a lead but that something had come up and he needed Jacob to take it over. Even though Jacob wanted to say something to Fred about what had been going on with the overlap between him and Fred, he simply agreed to take the lead and moved on. But when he followed up with Fred to get the information he needed so he could properly work the lead, Fred was vague and it was a struggle to get even the slightest bit of what was needed. Jacob became angry because he knew that if Fred would have let him take this lead from the beginning and do the job he was hired to do he could do his work successfully.

After successfully closing the deal, despite coming in midway and feeling frustrated about not being given the opportunity to do his job at the outset, Jacob decided it would be best to talk to Fred and explain how hindered he felt by Fred only partly delegating responsibility to him. The conversation went well and Fred agreed to do a better job of letting go and allowing Jacob to do the job he was hired to do. Unfortunately, though, instead of stepping back Fred continued to involve himself in areas that were under Jacob's purview, leading to Jacob feeling undervalued, mistrusted, and doing more work than was necessary just to keep up with Fred's interferences.

Beth was experiencing similar situations. She had changed the bookkeeping process to be more inline and compliant with what the accountant wanted. She had updated Fred on the process so that he would be prepared in the event of an emergency or if she went on vacation. On many occasions, however, Beth would access her accounting software and discover expenses that were mislabeled or even accounted for entirely incorrectly. She contacted Fred to find out why he had made these changes and asked why he didn't rely on her to do her job properly. Fred responded by saying, "This was an easy task and I didn't want to burden you." But just as he had done with Jacob, Fred was creating more work for Beth and also leaving her feeling frustrated, undervalued, and mistrusted. Fred's micromanaging and inability to let go were becoming a parasite that was infecting the health of his business.

After a few more months of Fred's interfering, Beth and Jacob decided to discuss with him how his actions were continuing to frustrate them as well as creating additional work for them. Instead of listening to his employees' valid concerns, Fred got defensive and retorted, "This is my company and I will run it the way I want." Shortly after that meeting Fred found himself looking for a new sales manager and bookkeeper because Jacob and Beth decided to move on to a company where they felt respected and listened to.

Fred started missing deadlines again, lost out on new business opportunities, and even lost some existing customers. By not letting go and inhibiting his employees from succeeding in their positions, Fred was effectively a parasite on his own business, killing it from the inside.

The Cure

There are two ways to grow a business—either through leadership or dictatorship. Both are effective, but only one yields a truly healthy business. The difference is that dictatorship is not scalable, and leadership is. A leadership mentality is about growing your business *past* you by enabling your employees to be successful in their positions, rather than having a mindset that it's all *about* you. A dictatorship mentality assumes that everything in the business depends on you as the owner. It is this mindset that actually ends up capping the business's growth potential.

As leaders, we have to empower our employees and allow them to succeed or fail forward—meaning that even when employees make mistakes there's a mindset around learning from the mistake and moving on from it, rather than letting the "failure" define the employee and their position. Great employees want to feel empowered and if they do, they will strive to succeed both for and with your business. If they feel micromanaged or distrusted in their positions, they will find a job at another company that does empower them. Business owners and leaders rob the business of its ability to grow past them and be successful when they employ the type of dictatorship mindset that Fred did.

When we see business owners struggling with letting go and who are working too much *in* their businesses when they should be working *on* it, we use a simple but effective method that both helps them identify what they should be doing and facilitates their delegation of tasks.

We start by listing each seat in the company, accompanied by a list of the top responsibilities for that seat. (Depending on the size of your company, some of these seats may be filled by the same person.) We then ask the owner to put a check mark next to each seat that involves tasks that they love doing and are good at. For anything that doesn't have a check mark next to it, we either create job descriptions and/or positions or move the task to another seat. Then, for each task under each seat, the owner creates three columns:

Column 1: Do it and don't tell me about it.

Column 2: Do it and tell me how you did it.

Column 3: Don't do it until we talk.

Applying this type of system builds trust and clarity. Employees are empowered to do their jobs successfully, everyone is clear about expectations and how to handle various situations that arise, and there's a system of checks and balances in place. If you are starting to do tasks that are the responsibility of one of your employees, they can come to you and point out that you're overstepping based on what you agreed on.

Creating and fostering a culture in which we delegate tasks and responsibilities, where everyone is clear about their roles and responsibilities, and where everyone feels respected and empowered, leads to a productive, growing, healthy business free from parasites.

Are You Destroying Employee Morale?

As business owners, we are entirely responsible for our business culture and our employees' morale. It's our job to simultaneously encourage *and* manage people and to do so in an environment that fosters growth and success. If we neglect this area or, worse, behave in a way that destroys employee morale, we are being a parasite on our business and are actively killing it.

We have traveled all across the country and encountered business owners who act like tyrants. They are mean to their employees, openly disrespect them, and constantly criticize them, creating an environment that employees don't want to be in, which often leads to high turnover. Don't destroy the morale of the people that care about you and want to be there for your business.

The Diagnosis

Walter was the type of leader who seemed like a gentle giant. He would flit around the office checking in on his staff and taking care of problems. At first glance, he appeared to be a person who cared deeply for everyone, which made others love to come to work for him. But, among his small staff of fewer than thirty employees, his turnover rate was pretty high. Something seemed off. Walter's genuine love for people included his customers, who he didn't want to disappoint. His passion for success and drive for perfection were unrivaled by anyone we had met. But it didn't take long to discover the reason for Walter's high turnover problem.

When a customer complaint came in, Walter went from a gentle giant to a tyrant. He quickly got upset and wanted to find the source of the problem so he could hold people accountable for their actions. Walter's desire for accountability was appropriate—but the way he handled it was not.

He found the employee responsible for the error and started off the conversation in a normal tone. But as the conversation progressed, so did his temper. Eventually it got to the point where Walter was yelling and threatening to fire the employee. Walter was apparently known for this type of behavior— for being negative and volatile—and many of his employees eventually tired of dealing with him and resigned, leading to a vicious cycle of high turnover, low employee morale, and a destructive corporate culture.

The Cure

There are two ways to compensate people: financial paychecks and emotional ones. When you fail to compensate your employees with both and have an environment of negativity, yelling, blame, and frustration, you are a parasite infecting your business. You must be uplifting with your words and support employee morale. When you use your words in a way that damages the morale and motivation of your employees, you're making your business sick.

There's a time and a place for discipline and accountability, which can be done constructively. Healthy conflict is good for business. As leaders, we must constantly strive to hand out emotional paychecks to our employees and lift them up so they—and the business—can succeed.

One way to foster employee morale and develop a healthy business culture is to take the time to have what we call town hall culture meetings, where you only give compliments. During this meeting, you publicly praise your employees for their successes, offer good news about the trajectory of the business, extend training opportunities, and foster collaboration. This is a very simple way to publicly show your staff that you care about them and believe in celebrating them.

We need to make sure that our staff is both held accountable *and* receiving praise for reaching the level of accomplishment that we have for them. These meetings will inevitably lead to a positive culture where success is on everyone's mind, and your employees will know that they are valued. As a result your staff—and your business—will thrive.

Are You Sharing a Clear Vision?

We frequently encounter entrepreneurs who are confused, frustrated, and feel like their businesses aren't running on all cylinders, but they can't identify why. When we ask them if they have a vision for their business, they typically have a vague idea, but not only is it not well documented, they have kept it to themselves. Having a vision and sharing it can contribute to a healthy culture and elevated employee morale.

It's your job as the business owner—whether you want it or not—to have a clear vision of where you want your business to go. It is also your responsibility to share it with your employees and your family. Sharing the vision helps with staying accountable—to yourself and the vision for the business—and it also motivates people to get and stay excited about where the business is going. Without a clear vision that everyone knows about and is excited about, frustration and confusion can infect your business. What's worse, the parasite is you.

The Diagnosis

When we don't have and share a clear vision with our employees, they can wander around like they're in a maze, unsure of what steps to take or the direction they're going in. Every year we go to a corn maze at a local farm in our area. And year after year, we started to see a pattern emerge that is a great analogy for what it's like to work with someone and be a part of a company that lacks a clear vision. One year in particular really stuck with us.

We spotted a mom with a few kids—one was running around and another was in a stroller. They were all ambitious about mastering the maze and excited to be there. Their energy was high, the goal seemed clear, and everything was in order. What could go wrong?

Eventually, though, they started to get tired and frustrated by walking down dead-end after dead-end with no clear way to get out. One of the kids was losing focus and was picking the corn and throwing the cobs everywhere. The other had dropped its cup and was crying, and Mom was trying to corral them and tend to them all while still trying to get out. Mom looked frantic and the kids were no longer having a great time.

Finally, Susan went up to the frustrated and overwhelmed woman who was nearing tears and handed her the map we'd grabbed at the beginning of the maze, which charts the course to the exit. Sometimes there's a guide in a watchtower above the maze, and all you have to do is look up and ask for directions. So there are options for help, but you have to know where to look and when we're at our most frustrated we're also likely to be at our least rational. The woman was incredibly grateful for the map. Once she was given the directions, she successfully made her way through the maze to the respite of the car and, likely, naptime.

But that year we also saw a different course. We noticed a mom whose desperation completely overtook her. Before we could reach her to help her, she did the only thing she must have thought was left for her to do—she took her stroller and her kids and busted right through the walls of the maze, leaving a giant hole behind her. She was just done and didn't care where she ended up, as long as she was out of that seemingly impossible maze.

The Cure

Without having or sharing a clear vision, you and your employees are simply stumbling through this maze called business. But instead of growing successfully and reaching your goals, you've fostered an environment of frustration and uncertainty, which leads to people finally reaching a breaking point and taking whatever exit they can find, leaving huge holes in your workforce when they do.

In order to avoid feeling like you, your employees, and your business are aimlessly wandering around in a maze, we suggest using the PLAN AHEAD method to structure your vision, which you can then share with others. We always say that if you fail to plan, then you plan to fail. It is our job as leaders to chart the course and create a plan that leads to the desired state of our businesses.

PREDETERMINE a course of action
LAYOUT your goals
ADJUST your priorities
NOTIFY key personnel

ALLOW time for acceptance
HEAD into action
EXPECT problems
ALWAYS point to success
DAILY review your plan

Once you've completed your vision plan and have communicated it to your staff, customers, and your overall network, you will find that others begin working for the vision and promoting your business to others. People love to refer a value-based business to others and employees love to be a part of a business with a purpose, cause, and passion to do something bigger than just making money. If you don't have a clear vision for your business, it's time to create one now and then share it with the people around you. If you don't, you are effectively making your business sick by letting it flounder directionless. Speak your vision, write it down, and share it.

Are You Elevating Head Count Above Heart Count?

When we elevate head count above what we call *heart count*, we can become parasites that negatively affect the health of our business. So what do we mean by heart count?

Each of our employees has the opportunity to work wherever they want—they choose to be with us and we must never lose sight of that. When we hire people solely because we need to fill a seat in our business, we elevate head count above heart count. When we concern ourselves with the heart count of our employees, we are looking to place employees in positions that they love and are good at, which in turn gives them energy. It is our responsibility to protect that energy. So our business's heart count refers to employees who are in positions they are best suited for, instead of just in positions in which they take up space and merely do a job.

When people sit in positions that fulfill them and give them the opportunity to use their skills and talents on tasks they love doing and are good at, they will have energy. And energy is the fuel that propels your business toward growth and success. Likewise, if your employees are doing the tasks that you are *not* good at or don't like doing, *you* will have more energy both for the tasks and responsibilities you love and are good at, but also for your family, your friends, and your personal life. This enables you to be a great leader, and you'll have more time to hand out the emotional paychecks your employees need for sustainment and which protect their energy.

When you invest in your business's heart count, the return is an increase in energy from everyone involved, a culture of giving and collaboration, and more time for everyone to do what they love.

The Diagnosis

Jamie wasn't your typical employee. She loved her job and was always willing to give of her time and effort to bring value to her co-workers, her boss, and to contribute positively to the culture. She often went above and beyond what was asked of her, simply because she believed in the work she was doing and wanted to be helpful and maintain a team mindset. Jamie did all of this because that's the type of person she was. She didn't ask for anything other than a little bit of validation that she was doing the right things at the right time.

Jamie's boss, Todd, was very much a numbers person. He was focused solely on the business running and making money and didn't take the time or energy to thank people for a job well done. Todd never vocalized his appreciation for his staff. When Jamie asked him if he was happy with her work, he simply responded with, "That's what I hired you to do." For the most part Jamie tried to let this roll off her back, even though she really would have appreciated hearing that what she was doing was at the very least satisfactory.

However, after three years of working for Todd and despite the fact that she loved her job and her coworkers Jamie found out about a position opening at a new company through a coworker who was leaving to join that company and who would be Jamie's boss there. Even though the position would pay a little bit less, Jamie resigned and accepted the position because she knew she would be working for people who were committed to appreciating the work of their employees. Todd didn't invest in or protect Jamie's energy and he lost her because of it. When I (Gary) was going through my illness, I saw my energy start to dwindle. Susan went out of her way to protect the limited energy I did have. At one point a doctor had told us that if I kept going the way that I was I would only have six months left to live. And I realized that this thing called time became very valuable to me. But another thing that became very precious was my energy. I realized that there are things in life—tasks and even people—that can steal your energy, making everything else harder and less joyful. So Susan protected my energy in the hopes of giving me more time. She made sure that I did things that I enjoyed, that kept me around people that I loved and who brought energy to me. Six months is a very short time and that limited energy that I had would have been consumed quicker if I was doing something that takes my energy from me. Though I'm grateful I didn't lose my life, I'm also grateful for the valuable lessons we learned about the relationship between health and energy and our responsibility to protect it.

The Cure

We need to make sure that we spend our lives in the areas of life that give us energy. It's our job as leaders to protect and preserve the energy of our staff—just as Susan did for me—to ensure that their time with our businesses is productive and healthy. There are two ways that we can protect the energy of our employees and ourselves while also investing in our business's heart count. The first is through our hiring process.

Often when we're looking to hire someone for a position, the job is based on those tasks and responsibilities we're not good at or don't like to do—that deplete our energy. During the interview we make sure the prospective employee is not only capable of filling the role, but that the role is one in which they will do things *they* love and are good at. We make clear what the expectations are, then take it one step further and ask about the prospective employee's *desire* to do the job. The conversation can go something like this:

"These are the things we need you to do. Do you understand these responsibilities and are you qualified to do the tasks?"

When they say yes, we follow up with another question, the answer to which is critical to investing in and protecting our business's heart count. "Here's the next thing. Do you *want* to perform these tasks?" The response we're looking for is one of excitement and passion. If we hear that excitement in their voice, we know we've found the right person for the job. At the end of the day, we want to protect our heart count by having people in seats they love, are good at, and which give them energy.

But it's just as important for us as owners and leaders to know what tasks we're good at and what we like to do. We need to make sure we spend our time in the areas of life which give us energy.

We use the acronym END to help us move through our task lists and determine those things that energize, neutralize, or de-energize us. END stands for:

Energize
Neutralize
De-energize (delete, delegate)

We use the letters "E," "N," and "D" as a valuation system on our task lists. If there's a task we want to do and that gives us energy, it gets an "E" next to it. If there's a task that neither gives nor takes energy then it's neutral and gets an "N" and we'll then later make the determination of whether or not we should do it or pass it on.

Then there's the last one. If there's a task that is de-energizing, we ask ourselves if it has to be done. If it doesn't really have to be done but just made its way onto the list, we delete it. If it's something that has to be done but we're not the best person to do it and the cost in terms of energy and time is too great, we put a "D" for delegate. We're going to assign that task to someone who will get energy from doing it.

When we as leaders delegate, we are then able to spend our time in our areas of what we call core excellence. If you're going home at night and you're too tired to play with and spend time with your kids or if your spouse or partner wants to go on a date and you don't have the energy, then you've probably spent your day doing things you're not good at and don't like doing, and it's stolen your energy from you. And the same is true for your staff. Investing in the heart count of your business is a two-pronged way to avoid becoming a parasite on your own business: you will have happy employees who are successful in their roles, and you will have more energy to do the things you love with people you love and who give you energy.

Are You Complacent?

Complacency is the death of success and it can show up and infect people at every level of business, from owners down to employees. This particular parasite is very damaging as it appears in numerous forms depending on where it's existing. But you can be sure that where complacency exists, there is a parasite that is destroying your business from the inside out.

There are a lot of reasons for complacency, among them are fear and a lack of balance. This can be fear of the unknown, fear of the future, and being too preoccupied with other parts of your life to be able to devote the energy that's required to continually be focused on growing your business.

One of the symptoms that indicates an owner or entrepreneur has become complacent is with the metrics of their business. They either don't track them properly or don't track them at all. The only metric they care about is whether they're making or losing money. But keep in mind: we can make money in an inefficient way. And numbers tell a story. They tell us whether or not we're being efficient, and whether or not we're maximizing our efforts. If you become complacent with your metrics, this shows that you have the parasite of complacency, which, if it remains untreated, will only lead to the death of your business. We always say you're either growing or dying. And if you've become complacent, then your business is definitely dying.

The Diagnosis

By all accounts, Nicole's business was successful. She was involved in numerous niches and on paper was financially sound. She always made payroll and could always pay her vendors. Her staff was happy and things seemed to be moving along just fine. Interestingly, Nicole had absolutely no idea about the actual financial state of her business. She simply chose to ignore looking closely at or making changes to her approach to her finances.

So how did she pay her bills? If the bank account got low, she would sell a property to make up the deficit or quickly broker a new deal to cover her expenses. She had no system in place to ensure her numbers were good or to see if she was capitalizing on her business successes. She turned a blind eye, was complacent with her metrics, and didn't push herself to find out why the bank account might be getting low in the first place.

When we started helping Nicole, we pushed her to look at all the areas where she'd been losing or wasting money. We challenged her to face her fears of not wanting to analyze her finances and to instead measure them so she could then be in control of them. Simply, we encouraged her to stop being complacent and to instead actively invest in the health of her business.

During our deep dive into her finances, we discovered two things which, had they gone unnoticed for much longer, could have led Nicole to financial ruin. The first was that we were able to show Nicole that she had lost a million dollars over the course of her business. When she realized she could have been a lot richer had she fought her complacency and actually looked at the numbers, Nicole had a complete mindset change.

Beyond that, though, we also discovered that one of Nicole's employees had been stealing from her, contributing an even larger loss over and above the million dollars.

Once Nicole could see the numbers, she realized she needed to watch every penny that came in and went out of the company. It wasn't enough for her anymore to just make payroll or have the sense that her finances were under control. She needed to know and committed that day to not becoming complacent again.

The Cure

What gets measured, gets done. We've heard this often and say it even more frequently because it's so true. If we don't measure the metrics of our businesses, we can become complacent about them. Once the complacency parasite sets in, it's just a matter of time before our businesses become too sick to survive.

As business owners, we must constantly ask ourselves, "Am I growing or am I dying?" The best way to determine the answer is to measure ourselves against ourselves to see if we're stagnating or hitting growth spurts. Regularly looking at key metrics keeps us as business owners engaged and focused, and constantly forces us to keep the mindset of "growing or dying" at the forefront. Every quarter we have to decide if we're playing offense or defense. Consistently making those decisions keeps us pushing in the right direction.

We've seen that people can get unfocused after ninety days, so we encourage business owners to create growth patterns to avoid this lack of focus so that they can continue to grow properly. Look at your KPIs and review them on a weekly basis. Be sure that every employee in your business is tied to either a revenue number or an expense number and review those metrics as well. Holding yourself accountable to reviewing your metrics weekly—with an eye toward a quarterly analysis—is the cure for complacency.

This review isn't just limited to our businesses, though. If we can measure where we were personally last quarter and compare it to where we are now, we will see those areas where we need more balance, more focus, and more energy. (We talk about strategies to get more balance in our lives on p. 94, in Part Three.)

If you're constantly looking at where you are and thinking about where you want to be, complacency won't become an issue because you'll always be striving toward growth and improvement. Complacency is the enemy of success. Accountability and focus are the enemies of complacency. And each day you get to choose.

Part Two

*Is Your Staff
The Parasite?*

Now that we have looked at whether or not you're being a parasite on your business, it's time to look at instances where your staff could be a parasite. It's important to be on the lookout for ways your staff—including your leadership team or business unit leaders as well as your employees—may be creating an environment that is causing your business to be sick.

Sometimes, as you'll see, your staff is reacting to something that's difficult, like change, and is being a parasite on your business because they're trying to figure out how to best navigate a situation that's confusing or uncomfortable. Other times there are more malicious behaviors that are breeding grounds for an unhealthy business environment. But most of the time these circumstances are only fatal to your business if they're left unchecked. Our goal is to help you diagnose the problem and provide you with the cure so that you can remedy the situation in a positive and healthy way so your business and your staff can get back on track.

Is Your Staff Complacent?

As we've mentioned, complacency can infect your business at every level, and your staff is no exception. It's worth repeating—complacency is the death of success. Some symptoms of your staff becoming complacent are when they get so stuck in the day-to-day routine that they stop being innovative, they stop asking why, and they stop challenging themselves and those around them. Processes can become one of the most neglected parts of a businesses and it is in this area where complacency shows up most readily.

If you don't create focus around your processes—and the people involved in them—your staff can fall into a complacency mindset and the health of your businesses will suffer dramatically. Asking why and listening closely for the answer is a great way to see if the parasite of complacency has taken hold and will then allow you to develop systems that will combat that common parasite.

The Diagnosis

At one point a client brought us in to analyze their company's processes. When it came time to review the bill pay process, we asked the finance department and the mailroom employees to sit in with us. We started by reviewing how the mail and invoices were received. The mailroom department head, Linda, said, "As soon as we get an invoice, we open the invoice for finance."

As we always do when we process map, we asked why. "Why is the mail room opening the finance department's mail?"

"I'm not sure. We were told to do that and it's the way we've always done it," Linda replied.

Whenever we hear, "We've always done it this way," or even simply hear, "I don't know" when we ask the question why, we immediately know we're dealing with complacency.

Then we asked the finance department head, Chloe, "Why is Linda opening your mail?" She said she didn't know. We continued asking questions to get to the root of the process and to unearth where the complacency began.

"So, Linda, what do you do with the mail when you open it?"

"I index it and put it on a spreadsheet," she said.

"Why?" we asked.

"I was told finance needed me to do that so they would have a quick reference to it."

We turned back to Chloe. "Why do you need this quick reference?"

"I don't!" she exclaimed. "We needed that process for a week fifteen years ago when we were being audited!"

So for fifteen years, a process was being done that was not only unnecessary but also time-consuming, confusing, and was leading to larger problems, which we were about to discover had huge repercussions.

We wanted to fully represent the cost of becoming complacent so we continued our questions. We asked Linda on average how long it took her to do this process each week and she said between fifteen and twenty hours. After some more questions, we came to discover that, based on Linda's salary and how many hours it took her each week to do this unnecessary task, this complacency had cost the company about a quarter of a million dollars over the course of fifteen years. Not only was the broken process revealed, but the true monetary cost of complacency was also shown for the parasite that it is.

The Cure

When we as owners fail to challenge the status quo in our businesses, the result can be that complacency sets in among our staff. As shown in the story above, when you ask a question and you are met with a dismissive or vague response or you're told that's just how it's always been done, that's a symptom of the parasite of complacency.

One of the immediate ways to overcome this is to start identifying opportunities for challenging the status quo. Think about your workplace for a minute. Picture the status quo. Ask yourself, "What would I change right now?" What are some problem areas that immediately come to mind? Break this down even further and think of areas of inefficiency that are affecting your processes, your people, your productivity, and your profitability. Identifying these areas of complacency can help you overcome it. We can't fix what we don't look at and identify.

Once you've identified some of these problem areas as you see them, start to hold discovery sessions with the people involved in those areas. These sessions are meant to remedy the problem and get your business healthy again. The best way to do that is to be clear from the outset that the purpose of these meetings is to heal and grow and to challenge the status quo. Clearly communicate to the participants that *anyone* on the team can challenge the status quo. This is a critical ingredient of a healthy culture and you must establish this spirit of collaboration and challenge so your business and its people can thrive. We always say that ten people's ideas are better than that of one. Be sure to recognize and acknowledge good ideas when they are offered.

At these discovery sessions, you have to be sure to ask the right question. As you're looking at whatever problem areas where you've seen complacency take hold, you have to ask the question why. Asking why gets to the root cause of the problem and we have found that it takes asking why seven times to really get deep enough to find the root cause of where a problem or confusion has originated. Once you've discovered the root cause, you can immediately set to work establishing new, better, and healthier processes because you'll have challenged the status quo, you'll have enhanced collaboration and communication among your staff, and you'll be back on your way toward having a healthy and thriving business that is no longer infected by the parasite of complacency.

Is Your Staff Resistant?

Managing and instituting change are ongoing and necessary parts of running and growing your business. And your staff is a big contributor to the success of that change. If you see resistance among your staff in the face of change, then that means your business is being infected by the parasite of poorly managed changes—your staff's resistance is the *symptom* of that poorly managed change. It is always difficult to challenge the status quo or make a change in your company, but there are ways to be prepared for and effectively manage change so that your staff doesn't resist in such a way as to cause real and permanent damage to your business and its culture.

There are two types of resistors we see in staff that are not handling change well: active and passive. Active resistors are openly defiant and very clear about their dislike for the change. They will talk about it with anyone who will listen and will often loudly complain and simply state that they won't do things the new way. Passive resistors are more subtle and can be more dangerous. They will agree to the change to your face, then simply not do what is necessary to help bring the change about. They will drag their feet, make excuses, and create an environment where other people will have to deal with their work that's not getting done.

A big part of having a resistant staff is that the changes you're seeking to implement aren't being managed as effectively as they could be. We put this parasite of resistance in the staffing section because if this situation is left unchecked, it can lead to myriad other problems with your staff, including the creation of silos, a toxic work environment, and your staff creating their own vision for the company separate from yours. So, if you are seeing resistance in your staff, it's not entirely a "people problem"—it's sometimes a poorly managed changed problem.

The Diagnosis

There was a company that was going through a buyout and they called us in to help them manage the process because things had gotten out of control. Of course a buyout is a confusing and chaotic time, but this had gotten to the point where it was almost unbearable and nothing was getting done. The business had essentially ground to a halt. They were having meeting after meeting trying to make the transition work, but things weren't moving forward and nobody knew what they were supposed to be doing.

During a town hall meeting, when one of the department heads, Michael, was briefing everyone on some changes that were coming to the processes in that department, an employee, Helen, stood up, interrupted her boss, and loudly exclaimed that she couldn't believe this was happening. She then very openly and defiantly said in front of everyone that she absolutely would not adopt the new process. Michael just wearily asked her to sit down. He didn't address her behavior or her emotions.

Helen insisted that she was being treated poorly and that she'd been at her job for a long time and had always done things a certain way, then reiterated that she would not adopt the new way. Helen even tried to incite unrest in some of the other employees, asking them pointedly if they were going to adopt the new way. Michael again just asked her to sit down, saying that he'd talk to her after the meeting to address her concerns. Instead of sitting down, however, Helen made a big deal about leaving in the middle of the meeting, actively resisting the change that was going on around her. Michael continued talking to a room full of shocked, uncomfortable, and thoroughly confused staff who didn't know who to listen to.

After that meeting, we went to sit in on a one-on-one meeting with Michael and another member of his staff, Mack. Michael had told us the purpose of this meeting was a follow-up with Mack, who was supposed to have completed some financial spreadsheets two weeks prior but had not. The spreadsheets themselves weren't a new task for Mack, rather it was the timing around them and who they were intended for (the new ownership). That day's meeting was to ensure that the spreadsheets that were already late at the previous meeting were now done.

Mack arrived at the meeting late. When Michael asked him about the status of the spreadsheets, Mack gave a number of excuses for why the work was still not done. Michael was clearly frustrated but seemed to be at a loss about what to do because the new owners needed the material. He finally told Mack to send him everything that he had done so that he could finish the work himself. Mack asked for another extension, this time blaming the chaos of the transition as the reason for why he hadn't been able to finish the work, but Michael said they were out of time and again insisted that he would finish them. Mack left the meeting with no disciplinary action, no plan for how to move ahead, and having effectively gotten out of doing work that was required of him, all because he passively resisted the changes that were being asked of him.

The Cure

Resistance is a natural attempt to slow things down to a point of manageability. Some people resist change just because it really is more work. And it is! During a change, people have to rethink every detail of how they do things, which is tiring, especially when they perceive that they are already working as hard as they can and yet are being asked to do more with less.

Many people resist change simply because they are not sure what they are supposed to be doing or how or when. It is your responsibility to make sure your staff understands that they have to say goodbye to the old way and begin to explore the opportunities of the new way, whether they feel they are completely ready or not. Just as human development follows a predictable, phased course, so do transitions and people's responses and reactions to them. Even resistance follows a predictable cycle. If each phase of the change is managed with knowledge and respect, people can master the tasks of that phase and move on to the next. If a phase is mismanaged with misinformation or lack of trust, people get stuck in it, which can have fatal effects on productivity.

You can't control people's behavior but you can mitigate their negative responses to change by managing it effectively and appropriately. The secret is not to brace yourself for change, but rather to loosen up and roll with the flow. Flexibility is one of the keys to being a good change agent. People resist what they don't understand. The first step to effectively manage change and avoid developing a resistant staff is for you to expect challenges. There's no way around it—change is difficult. Then, you must go through the necessary phases to ensure that the outcome is achieved as painlessly as possible, ensuring that everything is clearly communicated so there are as few surprises as possible. If you are an effective change manager then you can significantly reduce the resistance you experience from your staff.

It's important for you as the leader or manager to understand the dynamics of change and what people go through as they experience it so that you are prepared to manage it effectively, quickly, and supportively. The following six dynamics are the essence of transition management. They are also the areas that allow you to measure your progress. As the changes are integrated, these six areas lose their disruptive effect and things return to normal. The dynamics of change are:

- Communications deteriorate: Lose touch
- Productivity suffers: Lose momentum
- Loss of team play: Lose sight of competitors
- Power/Turf struggles: Lose sight of customers
- Morale goes down: Lose commitment
- Bailouts occur: Lose good people

Now that you see what the dynamics of change are, you can be on the lookout for resistance among your staff. Not all resistance shows up the same way, as seen in the story above, and there are other symptoms of resistance that you should be aware of so that you can effectively deal with them. Keep in mind that active resistance may not always be a negative, and people who don't appear to be resisting may become your biggest problem. But knowing what you're looking for will help you promptly and effectively identify the behavior before it becomes a larger issue. Symptoms of active resistance are:

- Deliberate opposition
- Reduction in output
- Chronic quarrels
- Hostility
- Saying why the change won't work
- Agitating others
- Not reporting problems
- Problem denial

Symptoms of passive resistance are:

- Withholding information
- Foot-dragging
- No confrontation, but still no productivity
- Not attacking the solution, but not supporting it, either
- People saying, "We've always done it this way"
- Overcomplicating the new way

Being an effective change agent requires you to do some work on yourself as well. It's not just about managing your staff—you have to be able to control yourself and your emotions. During changes, your job gets more complex as well as that of your staff, but you will be better able to manage and support your staff if you are also prepared for what you need to do for your-self. As you manage both the change itself and the effects of it on your staff, you as the leader must:

- Control your attitude
- Take some ownership of the changes
- Choose your battles carefully
- Be tolerant of management mistakes

- Keep your sense of humor
- Avoid letting your strengths become your weaknesses
- Practice good stress management techniques
- Support higher management
- Invent the future instead of trying to redesign the past

Knowledge is power. Now that you can identify resistors and are clear on the dynamics of change, you can more effectively understand what you need to focus on during transitions or changes. The first step in managing change is to keep your priorities clear. Your priorities are what we call The Three P's—you are accountable for managing productivity, managing your people, and managing profits. Above all else, you must keep in mind that during a change or transition it is more important to the do the right things than it is do everything exactly right. If you keep The Three P's as your priorities, you will be doing the right things.

And, finally, you must communicate! We can't emphasize this enough. Communicate that the old way is gone. Communicate that the new way is here to stay. Communicate that you know this is difficult but that everyone will get through it together. Without communication, the losses to productivity, people, and profits can be fatal to your business. Below are some ways to effectively help your people as you manage whatever change your business is poised to make.

- Help Employees with the Ending
  - ❑ Emphasize the death of old ways
  - ❑ Promise change, do not promise a return to normalcy
  - ❑ Let them vent

- Help Employees with the Transition Phase
  - ❑ Keep them informed
  - ❑ Assign specific tasks with short timeframes
  - ❑ Raise standards of performance
  - ❑ Confront rebelliousness and active resistance with a bottom line of get with the program or get out

- Help Employees with the Beginning
  - ❑ Help them see that they have a new job and a new employer
  - ❑ Help them understand and commit to both their new job and new employer

Without change, businesses lose their ability to adapt to what happens around them in the social, political, technological, legal, and other environments. Change is a constant, unavoidable part of doing business. If you can effectively manage the changes that are inevitable in order for your business to succeed, you can avoid becoming infected with the parasite of a resistant staff. For your business to thrive and be healthy in all climates, you must be an effective change manager.

Is Your Staff Pushing Their Own Vision?

We discussed earlier the importance of having a vision for your company and speaking it. One of the many side effects of not doing this is that your staff—and your leaders, most specifically—may develop, push, and drive toward a vision *they* create, instead of working toward achieving the company's goals. This parasite of having leaders who push their own vision can make your business sick by causing confusion, affecting morale, having high turnover, and leading your company away from its goals instead of toward them. Remember, in the absence of a clear vision from you, your people will create their own.

The Diagnosis

Chris was an entrepreneur with a goal to grow his business to $2 million a year. Part of achieving that goal was hiring the right people in the right positions and making sure that they understood what their individual goals were as they related to the overall company objective. Chris brought on Kate, who he thought was a team player and someone who would share his vision with her subordinates. But this was not the case.

Instead of articulating Chris's vision, Kate did the opposite. She undermined his goal and told the employees that it wasn't achievable. She went behind Chris's back and told the employees that he wasn't looking out for their best interests and that if they wanted to keep their jobs they should do things her way. And since Chris hadn't clearly articulated his vision, didn't consistently speak it, and hadn't shared it with everyone in the company, the employees in Kate's department developed a loyalty to her because she at the very least appeared to be on their side and looking out for them. Kate effectively infected Chris's business by sowing confusion and discontent within the workforce.

Eventually, Kate took the staff that Chris had hired and developed and started her own business, which was almost immediately successful since she stole his people, processes, and systems. Because Chris didn't constantly speak his vision for the company and share it with everyone at every level, Kate was able to infect his workforce, push her own vision, and cause massive destruction to Chris's business. The employees had nothing to compare Kate's vision against, so they followed the person who seemed to have the clearest idea of where they were going.

The Cure

There are a few ways to deal with leaders who are pushing their own vision. The first piece we're going to address is how to prevent this happening in the first place. We can't emphasize enough how important it is for entrepreneurs and business owners to have and speak their vision *and* share it with the company, for so many reasons. A vision that is written and not spoken is dead. And when you don't have one at all, people are going to latch onto something, which can give parasitic leaders with bad intent like Kate the perfect opportunity to capitalize on your confused workforce. If you don't speak and push your vision, someone else will.

Taking this one step further, since the employees in the anecdote above had nothing to compare Kate's directions against, they felt like they had no choice but to follow her. If there had been a clearly articulated and commonly shared vision, Kate's insidious behavior would have stood out as going against the owner's objectives and someone could have spoken up.

One of the ways you can be sure to speak your vision is through what we call weekly town hall meetings, which provide the time and opportunity for you to give an update on the current state of the business. This update includes articulating where you are currently with your business to ensure that it matches up with your vision for where you want to be. This type of meeting also lends itself well for motivating and inspiring your workforce by sharing what the business has accomplished to that point, again as it relates to the overall vision. This constant reminder of your vision keeps people engaged and excited and serves to effectively counter someone like Kate trying to inflict their vision on your company.

If Chris had implemented these types of meetings, Kate's behavior would have been obvious. The fact that she had different plans for the company would have stuck out as being absolutely counter and destructive. Had there been a spoken vision, when Kate started telling people to do things differently than how Chris wanted them done, the employees would have *known* that Kate wasn't pushing the company objective and her attempts to overturn and take the staff with her would have been futile. The staff would have been clear about where they were going and why they were doing what they were doing, and Kate would have worked herself out of the company because no one would have gotten on board with her.

Speaking your vision yields accountability in both you and the people around you who hear you say it. If you're pouring your vision into your people, they will identify when someone is pushing against it in the wrong way and parasites like Kate would never get to the level of damage that she achieved. In the event that you do accidentally hire someone like Kate, having a spoken vision will serve to mitigate the damage she can do—often, you won't even have to fire someone like her, they'll leave on their own because they can't push their vision on your staff and they'll know they don't belong. In the event that you do need to terminate a parasitic leader like Kate, doing so when you've had your vision clearly spoken and shared serves to further show your workforce that you are sincere about the integrity of your company and preserving a culture of teamwork and growth.

Your best defense against a parasite like Kate who's pushing her own vision is to have your own vision firmly in place and then to share it often and with everyone. Doing so creates a healthy, motivated work environment where everyone's goals align and the objectives are clear, which can only lead to success—individually, collectively, and professionally.

Is Your Staff Creating Silos?

A silo is a self-sustaining unit that doesn't want to share or interact with other parts of your business. Leaders who create silos can be catastrophic to the health of your business. Solid communication and a clear understanding of the role of a business's major functions help to eliminate this parasite.

When we go into a company and we hear a chorus of, "Oh, that's not my job," we immediately know we're seeing the parasite of a company having silos. We see this a lot when the three major functions of a business—sales and marketing, operations, and finance—don't communicate well with each other. What this leads to is a group of people who are not always acting in the best interest of the business, and instead are only focused on their immediate tasks and the success of their specific departments. While this sense of accountability and loyalty toward a department isn't entirely bad, it can become detrimental when this lack of communication leads to confusion and no teamwork, and when the group in one department does not have a clear understanding of their role within the larger scope of the company.

Essentially, part of how silos are created is simply because there's a sense of the left hand not knowing what the right hand is doing. It is critical that your staff understands how their departments and the processes within them fit into the larger company processes. Without this understanding, department leaders create their own purpose or their own sense of importance to the organization, and the leaders of that department will then get everyone on their team aligned with them to push toward achieving that specific department goal, putting the importance of that division above the overall importance of the organization. The parasite of silos can infect your business and negatively impact productivity, clarity, and morale.

The Diagnosis

Betty was the unit leader for her company's finance department and was known to be good at her job. She made sure that the invoices were paid on time and that the processes within her department ran smoothly. But she was also known for not prioritizing helping anyone outside of her department. As we worked with her, it also became clear that she didn't understand how her department fit in with the overall business structure.

If someone came to her from another department to ask for something, she behaved as if she were being inconvenienced and would say something like, "I'll help you when my work is done," even if the request was a higher priority than her immediate department-specific task. Betty was so focused on the work of her department and what was directly in front of her that she didn't take into consideration what the company's larger priorities might be.

By creating a silo out of the finance department, she ensured the success of her department, which came at the detriment to the rest of the business. Her demeanor affected the morale of the leadership and staff in the other business functions and slowed down processes in other departments because she wasn't agile enough to respond when another task came along that took precedence over her "day in, day out" task management. Betty didn't have a giving spirit and never stopped to consider why she was doing what she was doing or how it affected the larger company processes and objectives.

The Cure

One of the most effective ways to cure the parasite of silos is to have trainings across departments to make sure that everyone in the organization understands how processes flow from one department to the next. This process mapping that we do with our clients almost always leads to a lightbulb going off and someone saying to another department leader, "I had no clue you did that!" once they see how each department affects and supports the others.

The other benefit of process mapping is that it starts to clear up confusion and inspires communication. As we continue to process map with our clients, the next outcome is that some department head will ask another why they do a particular task. The response is usually something like, "I do that because your department needs it," which is often met with a blank stare and the admission that, "No, my department doesn't need that at all."

These types of conversations are an excellent way to break down silos, to ensure clarity across the departments, and to analyze each process to ensure that it is actually necessary and effective, which leads to a further understanding of how the role of each department plays into the overall company objective.

It is imperative that everyone in the organization has a clear understanding of each other's roles and the overarching purpose that they're all driving toward. If you are seeing silos in your business and a lack of communication across your departments, you must immediately break them down and take the steps necessary to ensure that everyone understands that their role is not isolated but is in fact in support of all the other departments.

Another important factor to consider here is that silos can also be created because of a lack of team health. If people don't feel loyal to one another or have the sense that they're on a team, they'll work in isolation and only strive to achieve an immediate goal instead of the longer-term company objectives. So, you also must ensure that your department leaders have good team health and that people are getting along. There are a lot of team-building activities you can do to help your staff get to know one another better, including workshops where people talk about their strengths and weaknesses. You can also hold company outings, which give people an opportunity to mingle in an informal setting, or take time to celebrate birthdays. These are some small things that can be done to help people realize that they are a part of a bigger group—the company—and not just functioning within their department.

Another effective way to break down silos is to ensure that public praise is part of one of your meetings. (We typically discourage the owner from giving this praise unless it's to give a specific reward.) But what you as the owner can do is create an environment in your town hall meetings where department heads praise one another for their role in achieving a *company* win, not just a department success. It is your job as the business owner to make sure your staff knows when there has been a company win, as this will help people to see that they are a part of something bigger than just their department *and* that they had a role to play in the organization's success.

Taking that one step further, it's important to hold regular meetings where your business unit leaders come together in a team meeting type of setting in which each of them works together to reach the company's overarching goal or to solve a company-wide challenge. This ensures that your leadership team knows that they are a part of something beyond their department. That team mentality will trickle down from them to their staff in each unit. These types of meetings serve as a reminder that it's not just about them as individual department heads but it's about what everyone needs to do in order to win as a company.

Getting rid of the parasite of silos in your organization results in having a healthy workforce that understands how each process and department flows into the next and will lead to clear and effective communication across your business departments.

Is Your Staff Aligned
With Your Core Values?

Your core values are the anchors of your business. They are your non-negotiables about your culture and the types of people you want working for and with you. It is critical that your core values are protected and that you surround yourself with people who share them. If you don't, you will have people who can damage and infect your company and its culture.

Some examples of core values are integrity, teamwork, having a giving spirit, commitment, and accountability. As a business owner you must be sure that you're clear about what your core values are and do everything in your power to surround yourself with leaders who share them with you and, in turn, will share them with their staff. These non-negotiables serve to strengthen your business and make it unique. If you have leaders who don't align with your core values, their toxicity can infect your workforce and damage your company culture.

Think of your core values like a set of magnets—people whose core values align are typically going to be drawn to each other, like magnets. But think of what happens when you flip magnets over. The ends that should be magnetic end up repelling the other magnet. People who don't align with a company's core values tend to have that same repelling affect, pushing away the people they should be drawing to them. You do not want a leader in your company who is causing this type of opposition among your staff. If you don't take action, the health of your business could be in jeopardy.

The Diagnosis

Martin worked in the sales department at a big company in New York. His job was to win RFPs against competitors, and he was exceptional at it. His win-rate was very high and he was considered very successful in his position. But something interesting would happen when Martin arrived at the office. One by one, people would go to their offices and close their doors. Where just moments before people were collaborating and working well together, suddenly the office became quiet and interaction almost completely stopped.

Despite Martin's success in his position, he rubbed his colleagues and his staff the wrong way. He was the opposing end of the magnet. He got frustrated easily and people found him incredibly difficult to work with so they did everything they could to avoid him. And Martin did nothing to change his dynamic with his staff. Though he was amazing at his job, nobody could get along with him and we eventually had to terminate him, which was met with celebration by the rest of the staff. Keeping Martin, who was so severely infecting the culture, was doing far more damage than the good he did by being effective at his job.

Martin started working for a competitor and was very successful there as well, even taking some of our clients at that time. But we stayed focused on finding a replacement that not only could do Martin's job well, but who also aligned with our company's core value of teamwork. We were not going to let another parasite infect our culture and detract from the health of our business.

Eventually we hired Jeff, who exhibited all of the same work qualities that were attractive in Martin, with one major difference—Jeff was a team player. He had integrity and displayed loyalty and cohesion with the other employees. The staff rallied around Jeff. They were drawn to him because he shared their same core values. And when the staff discovered that Jeff would be going head to head with Martin on an RFP, they collaborated and worked even harder together to win it.

The Cure

The first step in bringing leaders into your company who align with your core values is making sure you as the owner have identified what they are. Remember, these are non-negotiables that, if violated, lead to serious consequences. It is your job as the owner to make sure you bring on people who align with your company's core values.

In the case of Martin, the only real solution was to move him on. He was not willing to change his behavior and he clearly did not align with the company's belief system of respect and teamwork. However, in some instances, some leaders may not necessarily align with a value, but they have the desire to. If you have a leader that isn't strong in a particular core value area, they can be worked with through training so they can improve. But you must be firm and vigilant about this improvement and put them on an action plan. If they don't improve sufficiently, they have to be moved on so that they don't infect the rest of your business with their resistance to or lack of alignment with your core values.

Is Your Staff Making Excuses?

Do you have an employee who is regularly late turning in their work and when they're asked about it, they always have an excuse ready? Do you notice that nowhere in their excuse is any level of accountability? If so, you have an employee who is being a parasite on your business.

If you are seeing an excuses problem among your employees, then you actually have an accountability problem. And if you have people that are creating excuses and you're not holding them accountable, you're basically giving them permission to fail. Having a lack of accountability can seriously infect your business and stunt its growth, affecting your culture, your productivity, and your bottom line.

The Diagnosis

Amanda was a team leader who, when she would hold meetings with her staff to get updates on their projects, was constantly being met with excuses about why things weren't being done. Her entire team was always ready with an excuse for why they hadn't met their KPI numbers, why they couldn't meet their ninety-day goals, and why they didn't hit their revenue targets.

Those excuses ranged from there not being enough resources or training available for her employees to succeed to her employees saying she was expecting too much from them. Even when Amanda tried to provide the resources or training her staff was telling her they needed, the excuses kept coming without productivity. At no point did any of her staff take accountability for why they were missing their goals, and that should have been the clue for Amanda to know that these were actually excuses and not legitimate concerns.

When we went in to help her, we noticed that her salespeople tried to sell us on all the reasons why they weren't doing what they were supposed to be doing, instead of doing their actual jobs. Another symptom of the parasite of excuses—selling the excuse instead of the solution.

The Cure

Part of Amanda's problem was certainly that her employees were giving excuses instead of solutions. But, more importantly, no one was being held accountable, and that was her larger parasite within her company.

Creating accountability eliminates excuses. One of the most effective ways to create accountability is by meeting with the employee who's giving the excuses about their underperformance and have them set their *own* goals. Having the employee take ownership for the goal enables them to be successful and creates accountability—they agreed that they would do the task, so they are accountable to themselves as well as to you.

What we do is sit down one-on-one with the employee and lay out what our expectations are for them. Then we ask if they can meet them. If they agree, they've made a commitment to be accountable. If they say no, we'll ask them what their threshold is for the goal or goals—meaning, what is their capacity for getting which tasks done. If they can justify their reasons for their threshold, then we'll agree to that. And, again, they've made a commitment and will now be holding themselves accountable as well, which is the key.

Through this process, everyone is clear about expectations, everyone has agreed that they are capable of the deliverable or task, and everyone is accountable. If the task is not met, there can be no excuse—only a solution, because accountability has been created. If people are giving excuses and you're not holding them accountable for not meeting their goals or doing their tasks, you've basically given them permission to stagnate and fail. If we're not growing, we're dying, and excuses are usually the catalyst toward death.

Part Three

Are Distractions
The Parasite?

Not all parasites that we see in business are "people-problems." Over the years we've seen various distractions in myriad forms manifest as symptoms that can seriously thwart the success and health of a business. These distractions range from mind-set problems to more physical and immediate issues. Regardless, though, distractions can be a parasite on your business that can lead to serious complications and even the death of your business if they're not addressed and dealt with.

But, as with the other parasites we've looked at, none of these parasites have to be fatal. Some require more individual work than others, but all have a cure that, if willingly and appropriately applied, can lead you and your business back where you want to be—on the path toward health and success.

Is Fear Holding You Back?

There's a naturally occurring cycle that perpetuates when fear comes into our lives. Fear creates ingratitude, ingratitude creates entitlement, entitlement creates bitterness, bitterness creates silos, and silos create a lack of communication. We've seen it over and over, both personally and professionally, and this is why we need to discuss how fear can be a parasite that thwarts you and your business's growth and success.

The tricky thing about fear is that it doesn't always show up for us right away. It's usually an underlying emotion that affects our action, causing a lack of results or lack of productivity. People won't admit fear because of pride. We don't admit it because we don't want to address it. Instead, we'll use excuses as a way to avoid addressing the fears that are in our lives and which are holding us back. We always say that the hardest people to lead are ourselves. But before we have a right to lead others, we have to lead ourselves and that requires being honest about our fears so that we can either eliminate them or use them the right way. This isn't to say that fear is bad. It's just that it becomes a parasite when we don't acknowledge it, look at it, and learn what to do with it. If we don't do these things when it comes to our fears, we can become so paralyzed and infected by the parasite that is fear that we can't grow.

What's interesting about fear is that it can actually create a healthy respect for the thing or things we're afraid of. It can also create innovation and short-term vision, which is very actionable. But we have to first address it and ensure that we're not being paralyzed by it. We always say that fear either makes you do something or makes you not do something. How you handle the fear in your life determines whether or not it becomes a parasite that hinders your goals and makes you—and your business—sick.

The Diagnosis

One of my (Gary's) biggest fears is flying. I hate to fly, yet I've flown over 1,900 times in my life. This topic of fear is near and dear to my heart both because of my journey through Lyme disease and because of the ways I've seen fear manifest both in my own life and the lives of the people around me. What's most interesting about my fear of flying is that for the longest time, I didn't even know I was afraid. This story will be told from my perspective as a way to illustrate how the parasite of fear can creep in and lodge itself in our lives, hindering our ability to grow.

When I was twenty-three I was on a great path and doing pretty well professionally. Susan and I were married and we had our daughter, Annemarie. Occasionally my boss would come to me and offer me an opportunity to travel to meet with a client and, in so doing, grow both the company and my position within it. But each time he asked, I always came up with excuses to justify why I couldn't go. Finally, my boss addressed the problem he was seeing that I wasn't even aware of. He approached me one day and said, "Gary, I've given you ten opportunities to grow with the company and make more money and you keep turning them down. There's always a valid reason but, what are you afraid of?"

I was shocked. "What? I'm not afraid of anything!" I insisted.

"Well," he said, "there's something going on. Is it leaving your wife? Or maybe you don't want to go because you have a young daughter and you're scared of being away from her too much? What is it?"

"Nothing," I insisted again. When I thought about it, I knew Susan wouldn't mind if I traveled for work and I wasn't at all afraid of leaving my newborn in my wife's capable hands.

"If you come up with something, let me know so I can help you achieve without affecting whatever it is you're protecting," he finally said. But even following that conversation I couldn't figure out why I was never able to pursue the opportunities I was being presented with. A few weeks after that conversation, though, something very telling happened that opened my eyes to the real problem.

My boss came to me again and offered me an opportunity to meet with a client within driving distance of the office. He said I might have to spend the night and without hesitation I jumped at the chance. A look of surprise came over my boss's face, then he asked me, "Gary, are you afraid of flying?" Then it dawned on me.

"Yes, I guess I am," I finally admitted, both to him and to myself. I thought back to a terrible flight I'd had years before where we had encountered such bad turbulence that the flight attendant had hit her head and cut it. We'd been diverted and had to land elsewhere where I then had to get on a second plane, making the trip even longer and, frankly, more traumatic. The second time I flew was on 9/11. But until that moment I'd had no idea that I was so afraid of flying again that I was letting the fear paralyze me and inhibit my growth, personally and professionally. I hadn't let the fear resonate, so I couldn't acknowledge it or do anything about it. Instead, I made excuses and let my fear become a parasite in my life, robbing me of opportunity. I vowed then and there that I was never going to let that fear stop me again.

We see fear holding people back in our coaching work all the time. And probably the most insidious part of crippling fear is that, just like with my fear of flying, we don't always know it's there and taking a toll.

Noah was by all accounts a successful entrepreneur. His business was viable and sustaining itself, but he could not get past the sustainment phase and into a growth phase. He reached out to us for help propelling his business to the next level. After we talked for a while, we realized that he was offering a lot of excuses as to why his business wasn't growing, which all seemed very justifiable and reasonable, but we could see that they weren't the root cause of his lack of growth. He kept asking why he hadn't been able to really grow a business and see it actually succeed. He mentioned briefly and quickly at one point that he was afraid of losing everything, but quickly moved on to what he thought were the reasons for his lack of growth.

After a few minutes of listening to him, we stopped him and pointedly asked, "What are you afraid of?" His response was the same as mine when my boss asked me. He insisted that he wasn't afraid of anything.

"Well, you just mentioned that you were afraid of losing everything, so what are you really afraid of?" we asked again.

Noah thought for a minute and quietly said that he was afraid of not being able to take care of his family if something happened to him. In that moment we realized that Noah was holding himself back from growing because he was so afraid that if something happened to him while he was trying to expand he would leave his family with a lot of debt they wouldn't be able to manage without him. He didn't even realize that his failure to scale was entirely due to his fear. He had assumed that he was doing something tactically wrong or that he didn't have the right people around him or he wasn't motivated enough, none of which was true. They were just the excuses he was telling himself as the reason for why he wasn't scaling.

The Cure

The best way to combat fear is with knowledge, which sometimes requires a mindset shift. We are most afraid of things we don't understand. When we arm ourselves with knowledge, then we are prepared to work on and deal with the fear that's in our lives. But first we have to acknowledge that the fear exists, then we can acknowledge *what* we're afraid of so we can take the necessary steps to rise above and beyond it, either through eliminating it or using the fear to propel us forward. When fear is used properly it becomes a healthy respect. We can give our fears respect without allowing those fears to get to the point where they cripple us. Fear can be a great motivator when it's surrounded by the right knowledge.

The number one reason businesses fail to scale is fear, followed by a mindset problem, then connections (we don't know what we don't know if we don't know who we don't know), and then systems and processes. But, you can have the best systems and processes in the world and it won't make a bit of difference if you're afraid, which is what we discovered with Noah. He appeared to be doing everything right, but the parasite of fear had crept in and was paralyzing him. When we identify fear, we can remove the ceiling that's capping our growth.

So how do we heal from fear? Well, we have to identify it, respect it through knowledge, replace it with positive thoughts, and then innovate. One way we recommend doing this is through what we call a mental cleanse, which is an exercise we'll sometimes do with our clients (and is something we do every Friday).

Take ten minutes and write down all of your negative thoughts. This doesn't have to be pretty or logical, just open your mind and write down whatever comes up, including anything you're afraid of. Think about your business—where you are, where you want to be—and record every negative thought that comes to your mind. There's no wrong answer and you may even be surprised by what comes out. Noah told us that when he did the exercise he became completely overwhelmed with emotion by what he was writing because he was finally able to see the things that he'd been holding inside that he wasn't even aware of. And this speaks to the power of mindset. If we think our problems are because of one thing (like our employees or lack of processes), we feel okay. If we identify fear as being the problem, we can become paralyzed. Recording them allows us to free ourselves.

By purging the mind of the fears and anxieties it's holding onto, we create room for other things, namely knowledge and gratitude. When I (Gary) finally identified my fear of flying, Susan and I decided to educate ourselves about planes and air travel so I would know the truth. We studied turbulence and plane construction, for example, which helped me understand the technicalities in a way that felt more real than my irrational fear.

After you've written down all of your negative thoughts, get another sheet of paper and start writing down everything you're grateful for. This shift from the negative to the positive alters our perspective and allows us to also see those things that are good, positive, and beneficial in our lives that we may take for granted or simply not see because we're too busy being afraid or, worse, making excuses for our fears. By replacing fear with gratitude, we stop letting it dictate our moves and actions.

Finally, it's important to be innovative. Take a few minutes to identify the actions you would take if fear wasn't playing a role in whatever is holding you back. By identifying the actions you are being innovative, which will give you a clear purpose and momentum to push through if and when the fear tries to take hold again.

This exercise also lets you evaluate what fear is causing you to do or not do because you are being honest, acknowledging that not only the fear exists but also identifying what you're afraid of—and you can then decide what to do about it. This puts you more in control and eliminates the parasite of fear from crippling you and holding you back.

Are "Got a Minute Meetings" Distracting You?

Do you find yourself constantly being bombarded with "quick questions" from your employees and leadership team members? Are you being approached in the hallway or being interrupted by someone saying, "Hey, got a minute?" only to have that minute stretch on and on, without ever actually accomplishing anything? Do these "quick questions" lead to effective outcomes in a timely way? If not, then this inefficiency is being a parasite on your business and you need to eliminate it.

We define "Got a Minute Meetings" as an unplanned meeting interrupting someone's planned work. And we know that these conversations are rarely as short as one minute. In fact, based on some research we did, the average "Got a Minute Meeting" usually lasts longer than half an hour. And, to top it off, the desired outcome is rarely achieved, doubling the effects of the time wasted and strengthening the parasite.

The Diagnosis

We received a text from a prospective client we'd been waiting to hear from that read, "Hey, sorry it took me so long to get in touch with you. I just left a three-hour meeting."

We had to ask. "What kind of meeting lasts three hours?"

His response? "A very ineffective one."

When we dug a little deeper into the meeting, we discovered numerous things were going on that were major distractions and which were costing him greatly. First, the meeting had no agenda so no one was clear on what the outcome was supposed to be. Second, when we asked about who was in attendance, the participants ranged from the most entry-level employees to some of his company's top executives—most didn't need to be there and few got any value out of it. When we roughly calculated the salaries of the staff, ranging from $15 to $50/hour, and multiplied that by the three hours the meeting took, we were able to show him that that one meeting cost him almost $500. An expense he had nothing to show for.

And, finally, when we asked about the follow-up to the meeting, he didn't have an answer. There was no accountability put into place. We then discovered that what was supposed to have been a meeting intended to solve an issue (though no one knew that because there was no agenda) actually turned into the most dangerous and often most expensive drain in the form of a meeting—it became a discovery session, which we liken to a dinner date with a group of people.

We've all gone out to dinner with a group of people and sat around the table and watched the conversation drift into a series of complaints about this or that. Rarely is anyone trying to come up with a solution to whatever problem is being discussed and, more often than not, everyone is just piling on, adding their two cents and contributing only their experience with the topic. As we say, misery loves company. There's nothing wrong with this kind of conversation at dinner with friends and/or colleagues, but when your meetings become this type of back-and-forth complaining session, then you know you have a big problem that is costing you a lot of time, money, and energy.

This business owner knew that valuable time, resources, and energy were being wasted and he and his staff were being distracted by poorly run and seemingly never-ending meetings, but he didn't know how to turn this situation around and get rid of this parasite that was infecting his business's health.

The Cure

Needing to catch someone for a quick meeting is a part of the day-to-day operation of running a business. Situations arise unexpectedly that need to be dealt with outside of a formal lengthy staff meeting. But these "Got a Minute Meetings" become a parasite when they distract you and your staff, directing resources and energy away from the task at hand because they last far longer than they need to and rarely end up with a solution.

When handled correctly, most of these issues can be resolved in as few as five minutes. We've discovered that if there's no resolution after about five minutes, one of two things is usually taking place. The first is that a solution usually has been reached, but someone doesn't like it so they're politicking to get their way. At this point, the meeting needs to end with a leader making a concrete final decision without any further discussion. If you are the leader, then you can make the decision or, if there's a genuine need for follow-up, you clearly and concisely outline the next steps that need to be taken prior to that follow-up meeting.

The second thing that's usually happening if there's still no resolution after five minutes, is that there is not enough information to resolve the issue and the meeting has turned into a discovery session rather than being solution oriented. Again, it's your job as the leader to bring this to a close and schedule an actual discovery session where more information can be obtained within an allotted amount of time.

Instituting a "Got a Minute Meeting" process—and ensuring everyone is aware of the structure and implements it—effectively eliminates the parasite of what should be quick meetings turning into massive drains on time, energy, and resources.

The "Got a Minute Meeting Process" is as follows. The person who needs a minute should:

- be **prepared** to briefly and concisely explain the issue.
- articulate the **process** already undertaken to resolve the issue, including who was involved and what steps, if any, were taken toward resolution.
- have a clear **purpose** for the meeting's outcome, be it getting a decision one way or another on something they can't move forward on without approval or getting a concrete answer to a question they have tried to answer themselves and are unable to.

Creating and sticking to a "Got a Minute Meeting Process" does several beneficial things for your business, beyond saving time. You will find that the need for these types of meetings will decrease as people are able to solve many of the problems on their own simply by getting prepared to have the meeting in the first place. Secondly, the structure of the meeting creates accountability and empowers your employees and leadership team. People will feel supported and will experience the difference between being "led" versus being "managed" when they know they are empowered to solve problems on their own. And, finally, the process creates a space for people to grow and develop as individuals rather than always relying on collaboration to find an answer.

Having a "Got a Minute Meeting Process" protects the time and energy of you and your staff and ensures everyone is clear about their value, which will only enhance the health of your business—financially, energetically, and physically.

Are You Comparing Yourself?

We focus on others when we're unsure of what our future holds. When we don't see who we are going to be, then we look at other people to see who we want to be like. Have you ever been around a group of your peers and listened to them talk about their various successes and felt like you weren't measuring up? Comparing yourself and where you are with your business to where you perceive other people are is a parasite that distracts you from achieving your goals.

When we compare ourselves to other people and look outwardly to measure our successes, we lose sight of our purpose. The problem with comparing ourselves to others—beyond that it distracts us from pursuing our goals and objectives—is that it's futile and doesn't lead anywhere. To avoid comparing yourself to others, you need to evaluate and understand your purpose. When you're clear about your purpose, you won't become infected by the parasite of comparison because it simply doesn't matter how anyone else is doing—all that matters is how you're doing and where you're going, which enables you to focus on what you need to do to get there.

The Diagnosis

Rebekah was a business owner who frequently went to various networking events with other people in her industry. While Rebekah's business was doing well overall, she wasn't clear on exactly where she wanted to take it. When she was at one particular event, she overheard another attendee, Owen, talking about having launched his fiftieth successful business. She instantly felt inferior and like she and her business didn't measure up. There was no way she could launch a second business, let alone as many as Owen had. She compared herself against what she thought she knew about Owen and felt that she came up short.

Instead of benefiting from the event, she became distracted by what she perceived as her failings. She secluded herself from the group and didn't network or make connections like she normally would. All she could focus on was how successful Owen seemed and how much she wished she could be like him. She missed out on numerous opportunities to learn, grow, connect, and expand because she allowed the parasite of comparison to infect her and distract her from her purpose. What's worse, Rebekah didn't know Owen's purpose, which made her comparing herself against him even more unfair. Rebekah didn't even consider that she wasn't sure what she wanted out of her business or even *if* she wanted to expand and grow as Owen had. She just immediately compared herself to him, sight unseen.

What Rebekah didn't know was that Owen's goal in life was to give his money away to charities, and he launched all of his businesses with that goal in mind. Personal wealth wasn't his motivation or how he defined success. But Rebekah didn't see the results, she just saw the action—that is, all she heard was that he was successfully launching his fiftieth business, but she didn't know why. But, because Owen was clear about what his goals were and Rebekah wasn't, comparing herself to him was an unfair and inaccurate metric. We don't know what we don't know, so comparing ourselves to others is absolutely futile and only leads to frustration, negativity, and stagnation.

When our children, Annemarie and Jacob, were young and we would measure their heights, we never compared them to each other. We didn't say, "Oh, wow, Jacob grew two inches but Annemarie only grew one inch, she must be doing something wrong." That would be an inaccurate comparison because it's not in Annemarie's DNA to be as tall as Jacob. Instead, the better, more helpful, and more accurate metric is to compare the kids against their heights a year ago, and not against each other. The same is true in business when we compare ourselves to others.

The Cure

Matthew McConaughey said that his hero is himself ten years from now, and that's who he chases after and is the only person he compares himself to. Your only comparison should be against yourself as you constantly try to improve and get closer to achieving your goals and dreams.

The way to heal from the parasite of comparison is to be clear about your purpose, who you are, and what you want. If you find yourself infected with the parasite of comparison—or even if you haven't but you want to get some clarity about your purpose—we recommend doing the below beneficial exercise to help you chart your path and stay focused so you can get clarity and achieve *your* goals, instead of trying to be like someone else. We've done this exercise with ourselves, our clients, and even our children. It provides a really helpful visual and encourages you to evaluate yourself and gain some clarity, which is what will propel and motivate you when you're feeling uncertain and comparing yourself to others instead of looking inward to drive yourself forward. The exercise involves analyzing and writing down your core values, your focus, and your eulogy values.

Core Values

The first step in avoiding comparing yourself is to know yourself. Ask yourself who you are and what your core values are. Core values are personal nonnegotiable components of your individual value system that don't change. Our core values help to frame the lens through which we look at things. For me (Gary) my core values are belief, hard work, integrity, and giving back. Some of Susan's are perspective and positivity.

Knowing your core values also helps to guide you when you choose who to surround yourself with. For example, at the close of the first day of a multi-day training session, we always check in with the client. One day we asked how they were feeling and they answered that they didn't really get anything out of the day. So, we said, "Okay, thank you for the feedback. You don't know owe us anything but we won't be back." The client insisted that they wanted to continue but it was clear the relationship wasn't going to work since they didn't believe in the process and couldn't get past what they thought they knew. We chose not to do business with them because our core values didn't align and the exercise was going to be futile—they weren't going to get anything out of it and we weren't going to continue to spend time with someone who didn't believe in what we were doing. It's not a judgment on the person, it's just what is—a manifestation of our core values.

Write down your core values, be clear about them, and don't apologize for them. This will go a long way in helping you to avoid comparing yourself to other people because you'll have the perspective to be able to say, "Maybe they're where they are because they're doing something that doesn't align with my core values but does align with theirs." This perspective might help bring you closer to living your purpose.

Focus

Again, we focus on others when we're unclear about our own futures. But, when we're clear about our focus we can avoid becoming infected by the parasite of comparison because we know where we're going and we can focus on pursuing that purpose. To get clear about your focus answer the following questions:

- What is my purpose?
- What are my strengths?
- What do I love?
- What does the world need?
- What is my career/niche?

Comparing ourselves to another person when we don't know their purpose (like Rebekah did in the story above) or setting someone else's successes up as "better" than ours distracts us from pursuing our personal goals and objectives. Putting energy (which is a valuable resource) into evaluating someone else's successes and telling yourself you don't measure up detracts significantly from what you're capable of. Instead of letting the parasite of comparison creep in, compare yourself only against where you want to go and who you want to be and chase that. Having focus around your purpose will help propel you and allows you to avoid comparing yourself altogether.

Eulogy Values

If you could write your future story what would it look like? What do you aspire to be? We also call these aspirational values. As you answer these questions you can think in terms of what you want people to say about you when you're gone. Your actions today should be helping you get to where you aspire to be. Drilling down on your aspirational values will help you stay focused on achieving those goals and you won't get distracted by comparing yourself to others because you'll be focused on doing only those things that bring you closer to living your purpose.

When we outline and understand our goals, then we understand what we're doing, why we're doing them, and who we're doing it for. Having this clarity and focus leaves no room for the parasite of comparison to infect us because, frankly, what anyone else is doing doesn't matter. All that matters is that we are working to achieve and live our purpose.

Do You Lack Documented Processes?

We all want healthy businesses, and we need a plan to help us be healthy. Properly documenting our main processes allows our businesses to run without our involvement seventy percent of the time. The other thirty percent is why we have leadership and management. Imagine what could happen if everyone in your company knew what they were doing, when to do it, what the next steps were, and what the outcome should be. Think of how productive your business would be and how you would be free of constant interruptions and distractions so that you could innovate and work *on* your business instead of *in* it.

If you do have processes in place, do you revisit them to assess their efficacy and to get buy-in and feedback from the people who navigate them? It is not enough to simply have documented processes that sit on a shelf—they must be living documents that are constantly revisited and improved upon.

A lack of documented processes that are constantly revisited and improved upon is among the top four reasons businesses fail to scale. This is because this parasite of a lack of processes distracts you from achieving your overall goals and objectives because you're constantly being pulled back into the business, innovating on the fly because no one knows what they're doing. And, without properly documented processes, it's likely that your quality and productivity will suffer, which leads to more distractions as you deal with the consequences of that low quality and/or poor productivity.

Documenting processes stops interruptions because processes show the path and make it clear. Process mapping can take a seemingly complicated task and break it down into steps to follow on a map. It can also help create checklists for people to follow so items aren't missed.

When you document your processes you can get consistent outcomes because your staff and employees don't have to make it up as they go along or innovate every time they face a challenge or obstacle. Your employees' productivity is enhanced when you have solid documented processes and you are able to reduce redundancies, identify waste, and avoid expensive mistakes because everyone knows what to do and when to do it. When you take the time to process map your main processes and revisit them with the people involved, you can avoid becoming infected with this distracting parasite and keep your business healthy.

The Diagnosis

Sam owned an assembly plant that manufactured and shipped items nationally. He called us in because he was having problems with shipping empty cartons to his customers and he didn't know what to do about it. Orders would come in, the boxes were supposed to be filled from a conveyor belt, then shipped to the customer. Some customers were receiving empty boxes and were starting to complain. Sam's profits and productivity were way down and he was facing a shutdown of his business.

When we got there, we started to analyze the processes he was using—none of which were documented—to see if we could identify where waste was occurring. In doing this, we realized that there was no process in place to ensure that the boxes had been properly filled with the product before it was packed and shipped. We discussed possible solutions and told Sam we would return in a few months to check on how his company was doing.

When we went back, we saw that Sam had implemented a scale system to his conveyor belt process to ensure that each box was properly weighed before it was shipped. If an empty box reached the scale, an alarm would sound and a manager would go in and remove the box from the line before it could be shipped. The entire plant was constantly echoing with beeps, and though Sam's productivity went down due to the constant interruptions, his quality went up because his customers were no longer receiving empty boxes.

Suddenly and seemingly for no reason, a few months later Sam's productivity *and* profitability went up. He called us to come back again for another look and to do more work on processes with him. When we arrived in the warehouse, the first thing we noticed was that there was no more beeping. None. Instead, we heard a low humming noise. As we walked around the plant we saw huge fans set up everywhere and we just assumed that, since it was summer, the employees were hot. Then we noticed that many of the fans were pointing at the conveyor belt and there were empty boxes on the floor on the other side which one person was collecting and bringing back to the start of the belt. The staff had made an accidental yet entirely business-changing discovery.

At the start of the summer, the staff did indeed get the fans because they were hot. But, they realized that when the fans were pointed at the conveyor belt, the gusts would blow off any boxes that weren't filled. There were no beeps and no delays in the conveyor belt because empty boxes never reached the scale—they were blown off by the fans. And only one person was needed to collect the few boxes that didn't get filled and bring them back to the start of the belt. The staff had entirely reinvented the process, leading to healthy innovation, increased productivity, and increased profitability.

Now that Sam was familiar with the benefits of process mapping, he decided to have us review some of his other processes while we were there. We called in a number of his leadership staff that were involved in a particular process so we could see what steps they had all been doing to complete a certain high-level task. During that meeting, as we were getting feedback from everyone, we realized that during a particularly legally sensitive step, one of Sam's leaders, Lucas, was performing a task himself that really should have been done by an attorney. Lucas wasn't being malicious in his thinking; he had been trying to save the company money by doing the step himself without the aid of an attorney. But because no one had ever reviewed these processes together and no one involved really knew who was doing what, this potentially fatal mistake was overlooked. We immediately set to work process mapping so we could establish a process that was effective, streamlined, and legal.

The Cure

Our businesses can run efficiently when we have documented processes in place. The process is supposed to take care of the rule, enabling your leaders and managers to take care of the exceptions, which leads to a self-sustaining business. Without processes, you're constantly making things up as you go along and navigating redundant and unnecessary steps, which brings you as the owner back into the business to deal with things you shouldn't be. When you establish and review process steps with everyone involved, you get everyone's input and buy-in, which leads to the best results. With processes in place, you can get a consistent outcome every time and avoid redundant steps, which saves money, time, and energy.

Process mapping is the first step toward getting your processes documented, and you should do this at meetings we call Foundational Fridays. These meetings are specifically intended to create or review the foundations of your business. Keep in mind that process mapping has the following benefits:

- It ensures your organization does the process the same way every time.
- It improves employee productivity.
- It identifies steps that are *not* needed in the process.
- It removes steps that were created out of the mindset of complacency, because "We've always done it that way."
- It helps create checklists for each department.
- It helps identify where you can apply technology to streamline and automate your process.
- It allows you to work *on* the business and not *in* it, leading to a self-sustaining business.
- It gives you peace of mind knowing that everything is done the way you want it, consistently and proficiently.

If you don't have documented processes in place, the function of your first Foundational Friday meeting is to get your main processes out of your head and on paper. Be sure to include everyone involved in the process in those meetings. Doing so ensures that you find out how everyone has been completing the process and enables you to identify those steps that are necessary and, equally important, to weed out those steps that are wasteful and redundant.

As you approach the task of process mapping, be sure that your mindset is in the right place. Share your desired outcome with the people involved and keep the following in mind while you're developing your processes.

- Throw out all fixed ideas about how to do things. Don't come in with a pre-conceived notion about how to do things. Go through the entire process.
- Think of how the new method *will* work, not how it won't.
- Don't accept excuses. Totally deny the status quo and don't accept complacency when it comes to why things are currently being done the way that they are.
- Don't seek perfection on the first pass. Instead, be continually looking to improve.
- Correct mistakes the moment they are found. If someone is doing a process wrong make sure to communicate the correct way to complete it.
- Don't spend a lot of money on improvements. Throwing money at process changes is not always the best use of what we have.
- Processes give us a chance to use our brains. Get creative. The highest and best paid people are the ones who think for us.
- Ask why at least seven times until you find the root cause. People can waste their time and efforts on items that are not necessary all because no one asked, "Why are we doing it that way?"

- Ten people's ideas are better than one. Sometimes it takes someone who has no idea how to complete the process to see it objectively and to help simplify it.
- Improvement knows *no* limits. Continually improve your processes. When you've documented them once and have just put them on a shelf, they don't benefit anyone. Be consistent in reviewing the process to ensure it is still being followed and everyone is still doing it the same way.

When you can listen to how everyone has been doing things and then merge all of those steps, you will end up with a streamlined process that benefits everyone, eliminates repetition, enhances and makes more efficient existing steps, and adds steps that are necessary but that have been overlooked. Then you get buy-in from everyone and communicate the process externally.

But, as mentioned earlier, it's not enough to have processes in place and then shelve them. They must constantly be revisited and improved upon. If you have documented processes in place, then your Foundational Friday meetings are meant to ensure that the process still works for everyone involved and is leading to the best and most consistent outcome. Each Friday, you should be looking for waste in your processes. Check the following areas to ensure there's no waste as it relates to your processes.

- Motion: Excessive movement by people or machines
- Transportation: Product moving from person to person or between locations
- Overproduction: Producing more than is required at the current time

- Overprocessing: Unnecessary work beyond what is needed to meet customer requirements
- Waiting: Periods of inactivity while waiting for the next process step to begin
- Inventory: Unprocessed or partially processed materials or undelivered finished goods
- Defects: Process steps that result in scrap, rework, or re-processing
- Behavioral: Unused creativity and underutilized human capital

If you find waste in any of these areas, then you need to convert to a "Should Be" mentality, meaning that you should review your processes with an eye toward what you should be doing instead of what you currently are doing so that you can find the problem, eliminate the waste, re-create an effective process, gain buy-in again, and communicate the new process.

Part of keeping your business healthy and functional is ensuring that your processes are mapped out, documented, revisited, and communicated. Having effective processes frees you from the parasite of being distracted so that you can focus on growing your business and maintaining its health in all other areas.

Is Another Business Distracting You?

Sometimes it's helpful to think of your business like a tree. You plant the seed—the business idea—and you give it resources—time, money, energy, materials—so it will grow and thrive. The tree sprouts branches and creates fruit when it has all of the proper resources it needs, just like your business will grow and be healthy when it is getting everything it needs to be successful.

But sometimes entrepreneurs start to think that because they've done something great with their first business they should start a second one, which is not necessarily a bad thing to do. It becomes problematic, however, if you take resources that were meant for your first business and invest them into the second one when it's not strong enough to stand on its own. Taking resources that were meant for the first business and using them to grow the second can become a parasite because it distracts you from your initial goal and purpose and pulls resources away from the thriving core business, which could eventually lead to its failure because the resources that were fueling the first business are now being split and reallocated to the other. You're essentially robbing the resources from your core business which can lead to both businesses suffering. There are ways to successfully start or replant a second business, but it's critical that it be viable enough to stand on its own—to have its own roots and resources—and not be taking resources from the core business.

The Diagnosis

One time we went for a walk in the woods near our house and we noticed a big, beautiful tree that was growing at odd angles. As we got closer, though, we saw that it was starting to decay a little bit, despite its massive size. When we were finally close enough to touch it, we realized that it wasn't actually one tree but two—there was literally another tree growing off the base of the first. By the time we were that close we could see what we had missed from a distance. While the tree was still beautiful, it was showing signs of fatigue. Many of the branches on the first tree were dying and showing signs of decay. Some of the leaves were wilting or clinging to rotten, dead branches that were just waiting to fall in the next brisk breeze. The second tree was literally robbing the first tree of the very life it needed to sustain them both.

This is exactly what can happen when entrepreneurs plant a new business *in* their existing ones. Seeing these two trees got us thinking about the times we encounter entrepreneurs who have been infected with the parasite of a second business robbing resources from the first, distracting from it and eventually destroying it.

David was a real estate investor whose focus was buying and selling single family homes. His business was going very well and he had not only made a name for himself in the industry but he was also very successful financially. He decided to branch out into commercial real estate as a result of his success so he started to redirect money, staff, and time into the new business venture, thinking that his existing business could keep them both afloat and he'd save time and money by spreading his existing resources across the two businesses.

For a little while David's commercial business appeared to be thriving. He was able to make a few deals and things seemed to be going well. But David became so focused on the success of his new venture that he was spending less time in his core business. His staff was also spread thin trying to manage two businesses at the same time. David mistook what he perceived as the success of the new business as success overall, and he didn't realize that his main business had started to suffer. He wasn't making as many private real estate deals as he had before he started the commercial business. After a few months of being distracted by the commercial business and with his main business no longer able to sustain them both, David eventually had to shut down the commercial venture after taking a big loss.

The Cure

Let us be clear, we are in no way suggesting that starting a second business is a bad idea and we are not cautioning against doing so. What we are suggesting is that you protect yourself and your existing business and take the appropriate steps to thoughtfully and methodically start or replant a second business so that it will thrive and not be the equivalent of a sucker tree on your main business, distracting you and robbing you of the necessary resources required to keep your main business healthy. The mindset here is about making sure you're protecting the health of your core business. What do we mean by that? At the end of the day, any business that is surviving on the resources that it's robbing from your core business should be identified as a parasite. It needs to be transplanted into its own "soil" so it can grow on its own. That business should have its own resources, and that includes its own leader or CEO that is not *you.*

If you have a second business that needs to be replanted then a transition period and plan need to be put in place. You need to identify the resources required to make that transition and remove the second business from the core business, including the people, the money, and the time it's going to take. Part of what you need to identify is:

- Who's responsible for each part of the transplanting
- The measurement of each task
- The deadline for each task

Once you're clear about these crucial steps, then you must hold a weekly meeting where you review the status of the required steps and tasks and identify and solve any exceptions or challenges that come up. This is the process through which you will transition into transplanting the second business. But the timeline is also very important. Depending on the size of the second business, you may want to set a transition period timeline of three to six months. By six months, realistically, you should be able to make the determination of whether or not the second business is viable on its own. You can use what we call "Three to Thrive Metrics" to determine if your business is viable, which are:

- Good sales and marketing—there is interest from clients and/or customers
- The product is being produced and delivered—people are purchasing what you're selling and they like it
- Finances—there's a positive return

If at any point any of these three areas is struggling, you will need to make adjustments and then decide if the business should continue. This is the only way to ensure that the second business is not robbing resources from your core business.

You as the owner are of course involved in this transition period, but you should *not* be the CEO of both businesses. Once you've decided the second business is viable, you forfeit the right to be the CEO of it if you are still a resource in your core business. You must identify and bring in good people to lead and run the second business. It is no longer the responsibility of the core business to monitor the growth or lack of growth of the second business. The second business has got to be able to stand on its own at that point and be self-sustaining or it's going to falter and fail.

As entrepreneurs, it is so easy to spread ourselves too thin or to let our excitement and passion for something new distract us from our core business. But it is our duty to protect the integrity of our main business and to preserve the resources it is generating which are enabling it to thrive. If we get distracted by a second business and simply let it suck off the core one—like the sucker tree in the woods—eventually, the core business will not have the strength, resources, or energy to sustain them both. If you're inspired to start a second business, follow a plan, streamline the process, and preserve the resources that got you to the successful place that you are.

Is An Imbalanced Home Life Distracting You?

We often hear about how work imbalance affects home life. Articles, blog posts, and social media discussions cover the topic of achieving work/life balance. However, very little is mentioned about the negative affects an imbalanced home life can have on your work.

As entrepreneurs and business leaders, it's easy to get caught up in our businesses and neglect the other aspects of our lives until the issues there become so big that we can't help but spend enormous amounts of time, energy, and, sometimes, resources, resolving them. This can end up killing our business as we then neglect *it* while we're dealing with what is now a crisis and likely something that could have been mitigated or avoided altogether if we'd had better balance at home.

Taking the time to invest in a balanced home life—including your health and that of your partner, family, and friends—actually leads to increased productivity and focus at work.

The Diagnosis

Recently we were eating at a restaurant and the waitress was obviously having a bad day. Was this a bad day because of work or home? We didn't know, but what we did know was that she was not happy, which was evident in her service to our family.

Each of our requests was met with growing impatience. At one point she basically slammed one of our cups down after getting a refill.

When we got the bill, our son asked if we were going to leave a tip. After careful thought I (Gary) decided to tip her twice the total amount of the bill. We left the signed receipt on the table and proceeded toward the front of the restaurant, which took a minute because we had been seated way in the back. We were almost out the door when I heard someone call my name. We turned around to see our waitress transformed from an angry person to a regretful one, her eyes filled with tears.

"Why did you leave me this tip after the way I treated all of you?" she asked in disbelief.

"A mentor of mine once told me that there are good people, bad people, and good people having bad days, so be nice to everyone because you never know who's just having a bad day. I figured you could use a little encouragement," I told her.

She grabbed me and gave me a big hug and then proceeded to tell me how much the tip meant to her because she was struggling at home with her kids and her husband had recently left her.

The Cure

Being aware of the symptoms of an imbalanced home life—both in yourself and the people around you—will help you acknowledge the problems that are leading to lower productivity and which are taking a high emotional toll. Issues at home will rob us of our productivity and focus at work. What the above story illustrates on a basic level and what we have encountered at *every* level in businesses and organizations is that when people's capacities are taxed, their stress shows up in two ways and affects them on multiple levels: emotional and time.

- Emotional Capacity: When someone's emotional capacity is taxed, they get frustrated easier. They might act out with anger or withdraw from others. This is especially a problem if this frustration is taken out on customers.

- Time Capacity: When someone's time capacity is taxed, we'll see tardiness, excessive absenteeism, and disability claims. These are just a few indicators that point toward imbalance. Other signs not always recognized according to the American Psychological Association include headaches, lack of concentration, and irritability.

"You've got to work on you first." We've all heard this before, but how often do we apply it? When we get so busy trying to keep our heads above water and keep our businesses afloat, often the first thing to fall by the wayside is taking care of ourselves and finding balance in the other parts of our lives. But just like when we're on a plane and we're told to put our own masks on before we help someone else, we can't be good for anyone else if we're spreading ourselves too thin and not taking care of ourselves first.

Bringing balance at home starts with a philosophy that creates focus around a method called "Three to Thrive."

1) Meet with your family to determine *one* thing you are going to try and work on this quarter and create action to improve at home.
2) Create three milestones that will help you achieve your one thing, clearly indicating who is responsible for what part.

3) Have a planned weekly meeting to review the status of each milestone.

When we have balance at home and in our relationships outside of work, then we can be more focused and productive when we are at work because everything else is taken care of and we have minimized distractions.

We all want balance and to be healthy, so we need to make sure that we're getting that balance in all aspects of our lives, including our spiritual lives, our emotional lives, our love lives, *and* work lives. We have taken the Three to Thrive concept even further in order to address all the aspects of our lives where we wish to have balance. We encourage you to find areas in your life where you can apply this Three to Thrive philosophy so that you can attain more balance and more health. We suggest:

- Go on three dates a week, one with your spouse/life partner, one with your kids, and one with your friends.
- Read three articles, books, or self-help content that helps you with your "one thing." This also includes a counseling session if you feel it's needed
- Go to three spiritual activities or services a week.
- Have three focused sessions a week that last forty-five minutes combined:
  o Take fifteen minutes to write down every negative thought you have.
  o Take the next fifteen minutes to write down everything you're thankful for.
  o Take the last fifteen minutes and write down your goals for the next week. If you follow the mindset here you will write down three weekly goals with three daily tasks to help you achieve the weekly goals.

The results of this focus will allow you to create balance and more focus when you're at home, allowing you to be more focused when you're at work. This will lead to better results, reduction in waste of time and materials, satisfied customers and co-workers, and, most importantly, a more satisfied you who is goal driven and healthy enough to help your business reach its full potential.

Closing Thoughts

We hope that you have found some helpful guidance, advice, and practices in our book through the diagnoses and cures we offer. Our goal has always been and continues to be to help businesses succeed, not just financially but in all the ways necessary to be truly healthy. We all want our businesses to be healthy. While this takes dedication, commitment, and perseverance, we believe it is the most rewarding work you'll ever face.

Having a healthy business doesn't have to be a dream. It is absolutely an attainable goal that results in spreading health, wellness, and positivity far beyond the confines of your business. What follows is something I (Gary) wrote in 2012 while I was battling Lyme disease. I keep these words in my phone so that I can reread them from time to time, which helps me stay focused on my purpose. We hope you find some encouragement in them and revisit them often for strength and inspiration.

It's not failure that most successful people fear, it's going through life and coming to the end and finding they never truly mattered!

Studies have shown that people look back on life and they regret what they didn't do. They don't regret the things they did wrong. No, they regret the things they didn't do at all. They regret the influences lost, the opportunities passed up, the dreams left unpursued. They mourn over the people not met, the relationships not cultivated, the statements not said.

You are here for a purpose, not to just exist. You were not meant to simply survive, work paycheck to paycheck, and make every day the same. You are not here to live out the boring monotony that most people call life. You are not even meant to prosper or become a success. No!

You were meant to believe, work hard, have integrity, and to give back. You were meant to leave a mark that will last far beyond your years! You were meant to make a difference! You were meant to matter! That is good success.

Stop simply thinking of what you could have done better. Instead consider how long what you are doing will make a difference!

What is your "why?" Why do you do what you do? What gets you out of bed in the morning? What keeps you going when the world around wants nothing more than to crush your dreams? What drives you to risk it all and pursue the impossible? Too many people live life with a reason that falls apart at the first sign of opposition. What is your cause for being here?

Now don't get me wrong, your "why" is not a solution to failure. You *will* fail. The road to success is scarred with the potholes of mistakes. No, failure will happen. But your belief, your "why," will carry you through.

Orville and Wilbur Wright pushed through several years of hard work and failed prototypes before they finally created a plane that could stay airborne.

Like their plane, you were meant to fly. Your "why" will make you soar. It will push you to greater heights than you have known. It will cause you to go farther and faster than you thought possible. You will deteriorate and fall apart if you choose to stay grounded.

The true mark of one's life is not the money acquired, the goods gathered, or the investments made. No, the true mark of a life is the influence left behind when your time is up. What will live on past your expiration date? What will carry on beyond you? What legacy will you leave? Who will live their life thanking God that you lived yours?

There is no reason to delay your "why." Remove the fear, ignore the doubt, fight through the struggle, and disregard the uncertainty. Replace them with belief, hard work, integrity, and giving back.

Suggestions for Further Reading

Below is a list of books that we have read over and over and that we love. We can't recommend these books highly enough as sources of wisdom, inspiration, and motivation. We offer them here, divided by theme, as a place to start if you are looking for other resources that will help you keep your business healthy.

Systems

Traction: Get a Grip in Your Business by Gino Wickman

The Advantage: Why Organizational Health Trumps Everything Else In Business by Patrick Lencioni

Leadership/Employees

The Go-Giver: A Little Story About A Powerful Business Idea by Bob Burg and John David Mann

The 21 Irrefutable Laws of Leadership: Follow Them And People Will Follow You by John Maxwell

Processes

Broken Windows, Broken Business: How The Smallest Remedies Reap The Biggest Rewards by Michael Levine

Who by Geoff Smart and Randy Street

Mindset

Do It Scared: Finding the Courage to Face Your Fears, Overcome Adversity, and Create a Life You Love by Ruth Soukup

Start With Why: How Great Leaders Inspire Everyone To Take Action by Simon Sinek

Acknowledgments

I would like to acknowledge the people in my life from a professional and personal perspective.

Personal: These are the people who believed in me and helped me the most through our hard times. When it felt like others were running from me these people seemed to run to me.

First, both of our parents, Gary and Ada Harper, along with Harvey and Dianne Robinson. They were there for us emotionally and financially even though they didn't have a lot. My kids, Annemarie and Jacob, for encouraging me to stay the course and "Keep Going." My sisters Jeananne, Tammy, and Cheryl for believing in me and loving me through these times. Jimmy and Danielle Vogel for the love and support that only comes from good friends. Keith and Michelle Cowling for pushing me to climb out of the hole I was in and for the spiritual hope I was missing. Jonathan Smith for the encouragement and creative ways to ensure we made extra money. James Woolsey for a listening ear and for calming leadership. John Pearson for providing for our needs in a time that seemed lost. Dave Douglas for countless hours of Bible studies that allowed me to stay the course. Mike and Sonya Streeter for treating me through this illness through many doctor's visits both at home and at their office, and tireless nights of research and hard work for proper treatments to ensure I stayed strong both physically and emotionally.

Professionally: These people picked me up and empowered me even when I didn't have much to give back. Wayne Sheaffer for investing in my knowledge of real estate. Eddie Wilson, Mike Hambright, and Jason Meadly for the connections and trust to connect me with others in their networks. Tom and Becky Olson for pushing me to start Sharper and help others. Max Keller for being my first client and then encouraging me to write this book while guiding me through many of these processes. Josh Belk and Paul Boyce for helping me build the foundations of the business. To all the clients who have allowed me to work with them and even refer me to others. Beth Wolfe and Austin McCurdy for trusting me and joining Sharper at the beginning and helping Susan and me build a solid foundation that we could be proud of.

Made in the USA
Monee, IL
18 February 2021